The Hippie Revival and Collected Writings

The Hippie Revival and Collected Writings

Forrest Rivers

ISBN: 1515396959
ISBN 13: 9781515396956

To Mother Earth for all her love, inspiration, and guidance
To Mom, Dad, and Lex for all their love and support over time
To Rose my kindred spirit and fellow soul traveler through eternity
To Abbie and Luna for their earthy wisdom
To Sean, Alex, Austin, Jamie and Julie for their dear friendship
To Myrtle a wise elder and a living inspiration to all
To all beings of the Earth who rejoice in the spirit of God

Native American Prayer
Oh, Great Spirit
Whose voice I hear in the winds,
And whose breath gives life to all the world,
hear me, I am small and weak,
I need your strength and wisdom.
Let me walk in beauty and make my eyes ever behold
the red and purple sunset.
Make my hands respect the things you have
made and my ears sharp to hear your voice.
Make me wise so that I may understand the things
you have taught my people.
Let me learn the lessons you have
hidden in every leaf and rock.
I seek strength, not to be greater than my brother,
but to fight my greatest enemy - myself.
Make me always ready to come to you
with clean hands and straight eyes.
So when life fades, as the fading sunset,
my Spirit may come to you without shame.
(Translated by Lakota Sioux Chief Yellow Lark in 1887)

"Early in the journey you wonder how long the journey
will take and whether you will make it in this lifetime.
Later you will see that where you are going is HERE
and you will arrive NOW... so you stop asking."

— RAM DASS

"Like every religion of the past we seek to find the Divinity within and to express this revelation in a life of glorification and the worship of God. These ancient goals we define in the metaphor of the present – turn on, tune in, drop out."

-TIMOTHY LEARY

"You are the eyes with which God looks, and the mind through which God understands itself."

-STEPHEN GASKIN

Table of Contents

Introduction

THE CULMINATION OF THESE COLLECTED writings embodies what I hope are the essential elements of the hippie spirit: peace, unity, and love. Though these precious ideals have been contaminated to some degree by the pervasive influence of mainstream culture, they are still very much alive in the hearts and souls of all beings. In fact, these cherished values are currently enjoying a revival of sorts. In the United States, and throughout much of the western world, people are beginning to re-awaken to the notion that a society built on consumerism and greed are morally repugnant. What people secretly yearn for is love; an unrelenting and unconditional kind of love. We all want an understanding of God (Christ, Jah, Buddha, Allah, The Great Mystery, Universe, Creator etc.) that reflects our own unique connection to IT. This existential search for meaning is the essence of being human.

In channeling this spirit, the following pages represent one writer's attempt to comprehend the divine nature of things. Like the original hippies of the 1960's and 70's, I share their vision of creating a spiritual society that rests on the core values of peace, love, and unity. In turn, each one of these is emphasized in the pages that follow. More specific hippie themes are additionally addressed in these writings. They include: the sacredness of the natural world, the use of psychedelics for personal insight, the commune as an alternative model of social organization, the intersection of social revolution and spirituality, and a questioning of the meaning behind progress. These writings are also something of an homage to the early hippies who dared to dream of a better and more peaceful world. Each of these values, however, are also re- conceptualized to fit into the unique context of today.

Unfortunately, many of the very issues that the early hippies tackled (like environmental degradation, war, and societal alienation) have only escalated since the 1980's. We now live in an age when global warming and nuclear contamination (see Fukushima) present dire threats to all inhabitants of Mother Earth. Thanks to militarized technologies (such as drone warfare) we have become increasingly desensitized to the horrors of war. A palpable wave of disillusionment, too, has swept over the people. The sense of "something is wrong" reflects our current obsession with the expansive world of digital technology. Despite its undeniable innovations and achievements, the Technological Revolution has, like the two major shifts before it[1], come with consequences. Some of which include: cultural homogenization and displacement, a reduction in personal autonomy and a general feeling (among many) of lacking a life purpose. In allowing ourselves to be seduced by exterior distractions, we have severed ourselves from spirit.

What can be done to reclaim our place in the Cosmos? We must turn inwards. There are multiple paths that return us to the depths of our souls. Sustained interactions with nature, meditation/prayer, and creative expression are just a few examples. The more time we spend on our iPhones and on Facebook, the less attention we devote to these soul enriching activities. There are in these writings an added sense of urgency to otherwise familiar themes. This does not mean, though, that all hope is lost. This work is informed by an unwavering optimism and a faith that the beauty of the human spirit will prevail over ego. My intent for this writing is to help inspire this same faith in others.

Finally, something must also be said about the philosophy of the Native Americans and their impact on my own personal belief system. Throughout this collection of writings, the reader will notice that I frequently reference the original peoples of North America. I do this for two reasons:

First, to honor the immense influence that Native American thought has had on the hippies. Conventional thinking holds that the birth of

---

1 The Agricultural and Industrial Revolutions

hippie dome arose from Beatnik culture. I think differently. To be sure, the Beatniks embodied the hippie spirit in both their commitments to non-conformity and existential exploration. The Native Americans are their true forerunners. One can certainly point out comparisons between the two groups. For example, Native Americans regard nature as sacred, as do the Hippies. Native Americans place great emphasis on the non-attachment to material goods. Hippies do as well. Native Americans work to achieve peace and harmony in their communities. This, too, is a Hippie ideal. The comparisons could go on.

Second, the Native Americans are an inspiration for the awakening of mankind. For who can serve as nobler leaders for change, than a people who have endured unbearable suffering but have maintained their faith in God? Despite Dominant Culture's attempt to whitewash Native American history and suppress their traditions, the legacy endures.

A brief and related anecdotal story:

On the day I was to write this introduction, my kindred spirit (Rose) brought me on a hike in Pisgah National Forest. However, this was to be no ordinary walk through the woods. She led me one mile off trail to a secluded location by a great waterfall. Next to this natural wonder was a small cave. Inside of it sat a beautiful large quartz crystal that the Cherokee once frequented on their vision quests. As legend has it, journeyers would hug the massive stone to open up their heart chakras. There huddled with Rose, I had the unforgettable opportunity to embrace this same sacred rock. Instantly, I felt the stone's radiant energy pulse through me. It felt like the heartbeat of the earth. This was among the most awesome experiences of my life. I hope that this same feeling of inspiration that I felt flows throughout the pages below.

Peace and Love,

Forrest Rivers

(The Blue Ridge Mountains, North Carolina)

The Hippie Revival

THE HIPPIES ARE IN THE midst of a great cultural revival. A re-awakening, of sorts, from a long hiatus. In truth the hippies never really "died;" they were just driven underground by the forces of mainstream culture[2] in the decades following the 1960's, or joined the very establishment that they once resisted. Still, some of the early hippies maintained the practice of their values in tight knit communities. For example, the men and women on The Farm (an intentional community in Summertown, Tennessee), have managed to hold onto their communal lifestyle and maintain their commitment to countless humanitarian causes.

The various symbols of the 1960's counterculture never burned out either. The image of reggae icon Bob Marley is as ubiquitous as ever. So much so that, in two years living on a college campus, I counted no less than 100 of his Posters on the walls of friends or acquaintances. Peace signs also remain in vogue, as the image appears on everything from shirts to backpacks and bumper stickers. Longhair and beards even enjoyed a brief resurgence in the Punk and Grunge Rock sub-cultures of the 1980's and 1990's. Of course, more people than ever were turned on to nature's herbal remedy, ganja. Now, one could make the case that the symbols of hippie culture have been badly commodified. Nevertheless, people are still drawn to them for a reason: they each speak to one's soul. The hippies didn't so much meet their demise; more like, their ideas lost temporary traction with the general population.

---

2 I use this phrase to refer to society's cultural architects and managers: Church, State, Big Business, and Academia.

Definition of a Hippie

In describing "hippies", Dominant Culture generally emphasizes their adherence to non-conformity. For example, the free dictionary defines a "hippie" as:

> **"A person who opposes and rejects many of the conventional standards and customs of society, especially one who advocates extreme liberalism in sociopolitical attitudes and lifestyles".**

By comparison, Webster Dictionary defines a "hippie" as follows: "

> **"A usually young person who rejects established social customs (such as by dressing in an unusual way, or living in a commune) and who opposes violence and war, especially: A young person in in the 1960's and 1970's".**

To be sure, hippies are non-conformists at heart. However, neither description captures the full meaning of hippiedom. For hippies are not simply non-conformists. They are people who have adopted a particular set of core values which have been ascribed, cultivated, and practiced for thousands of years. Many of these values have even been taught by some of the world's most enlightened spiritual beings, including: Buddha, Krishna, Jesus Christ, and the indigenous peoples of the world.

Accordingly, hippies strive to cultivate these values and practices from within:

- Personal liberation through inward reflection
- Creative expression
- Self-sufficiency
- Devotion to community
- Reverence for the Earth
- Support for the principle of non-violence
- A belief in the interrelation of God, Earth, and Mankind

We find that the hippie's core is firmly rooted in a spiritual foundation. Of course, this does not imply that hippies (as with all people) always follow these principles in practice. Rather, their inner conceptions of truth are steeped within the above value set. Viewed in this light, hippie non-conformity is a response to the (perceived) spiritual decay of the mainstream culture. The hippie aims at two things through non-conformity:

- To bring their inner and outer worlds into greater harmony
- To offer an alternative moral paradigm by which to live by

This brings us to a re-definition of the hippie.
A Hippie can be defined as:

"A person who tries to attain personal liberation through practicing the values of soulful expression, peace, charity, independence, and reverence for the Earth through love."

WHAT FACTOR(S) ACCOUNT FOR THE HIPPIE REVIVAL?

THE HIPPIE REVIVAL IN CONTEXT OF SPIRITUAL PROPHECIES

The hippies are enjoying resurgence due in no small part to a great spiritual shift underway. This moment of transformation was long ago prophesized by the Ancient Mayan people, the Tibetan Monks, and several native tribes of North America. Each mystic sect described the present years as an impactful moment for the planet. This era is to be a time when the collective consciousness of all life expands. In turn, this heightened awareness will usher in a new model of existence. Put in other words, these divine peoples believe that our planet will more closely align with the energy of the Infinite Source, what many call God. [3]

---

3 See Tom Kenyon and Lee Carroll's book <u>The Great Shift: Co-Creating a New World for 2012 and Beyond</u> for an in depth description of this New Age philosophy.

The compatibility of the hippies' spiritual message with these prophesies helps account for their revival. The hippies are re-surfacing to help play a role in the emergence of a new global consciousness.

THE HIPPIE REVIVAL AS FULFILLMENT OF A NATURAL COURSE

The renewed interests in hippie ideals are also attributed to the natural rhythms of history. In one sense, the history of mankind can be viewed as a tug of war between the two poles of human experience: the spirit and ego consciousness. The way of the spirit consciousness may be said to emphasize the values of peace and tranquility, freedom of expression, and the unity of all life. In contrast, the way of the ego may be said to promote just the opposite values: conflict and strife, coercion and domination, and the elevation of self above creation.

As the spiritual writer, Eckhart Tolle[4] maintains, our human family is currently trapped in the latter vision. A glance at mankind's relationship to the natural world would seem to confirm his point. A heavy dose of hubris seems to underlie our relationship to both the Earth and one another. It is indeed good news for the planet, that the pendulum is shifting back in the direction of spirit consciousness. This eternal process might also be described as our collective act of *becoming*; or that moment when we find our way out of the darkness and back into the light.

THE ROLE(S) OF INFORMATION TECHNOLOGY IN THE HIPPIE REVIVAL:

The information revolution has played a significant role in the present day revival of hippie culture. Spurred on by the rapid growth of tele-communications, people are being exposed to information that was once unattainable. The exposure to news on the Internet has proliferated a culture where people "have to know" what is going on, for the "news" is only one click away. Of course, the people are still fed the typical amalgamation of commercial programming that passes off as news, but

---

4 Eckhart Tolle. <u>A New Earth: Awakening to Your life's Purpose.</u>

the difference now is that alternative sources exist. Not surprisingly, the Internet is abounding with websites that expose government and corporate malfeasance, environmental degradation, and the corrupt practices of modern medicine. The availability of this information makes for a more informed and active population. The hippies owe a good part of their resurgence to the revolution in information technology. For they now have a powerful vehicle with which to share their criticisms of Dominant Culture.

Like the Agricultural and Industrial revolutions before it, the information age presents a dilemma for the people. The avenue of telecommunications has facilitated a world of vast and instant communication. Thus, allowing for an unlimited flow of news. However, the "information revolution" has also (indirectly) severed us from authentic human interaction. Those of us in the so-called "developed world" find that an increasing share of our daily interactions take place over these new forms of communication like cell phones, email, and over social media outlets such as Facebook. Some cultural observers, like writer Stephen Murche,[5] contend that the decline in meaningful interaction has left us feeling alienated and alone.

Sadly, our society is ill equipped to diagnose this sickness in spirit because the information age has also detached us from our true essence. We have become so consumed by the technological world, that we now experience great difficulty just sitting still with our thoughts. Comedian, Louis C.K., hilariously captured this reality in a short segment on the Conan O'Brien show. CK cynically joked, that we would rather risk taking life by texting on our cell phones while driving, than engage in meaningful self-reflection. According to the comedian, we do so because we fear what it means to acknowledge our suffering.

This detachment, from both ourselves and others, has been further exasperated by our culture's continuous shift away from the natural world. This has only added to our sense of alienation. The feeling of emptiness that gnaws at the root of our society partly explains the

---

5 Stephen Munche. "Is Facebook Making Us Lonely?" Atlantic Magazine. May, 2012.

renewed interest in hippie ideals, for their philosophy coincides with the inspiring vision of spirit.

The Hippie Revival Driven by a Loss of Faith in Societal Institutions

The "hippie revival" is also a positive consequence of our loss of trust in societal structures. When one loses faith, the search for alternatives follows. In an insightful April, 2012 article by the Atlantic, journalists Ron Fournier and Sophie Quinton walk the reader through Americans' declining faith in societal institutions. The authors cited some of the following statistics derived from Gallup Polls:

- 7 out of 10 Americans believe the country is on the wrong track
- 8 out of 10 Americans are dissatisfied with the way the nation is governed
- 2 out of 10 Americans trust financial and banking institutions
- 2 out of 10 Americans have trust in Big Business/corporations
- Less than 50 % of Americans have a "great deal" of confidence in organized religion
- The same figure has a "great deal" of confidence in the public education system
- And according to a June, 2013 Gallup poll less than 1 in 4 Americans trust major newspapers and television news sources

Most significantly, the article suggests that unbridled greed and commercialism – along with the disruptive currents of the technological revolution – have led to this loss of faith. This dwindling trust even extends to organized religion, which has been ill equipped to address the great changes of the times. From this perspective, it is easy to see why the hippie philosophy appeals to the population. Many people would prefer an alternative to a hyper-commercialized society.

Signs That Point to the Hippie Revival

Support for the Commune

A surge in the popularity of communes is among the most convincing signs that point to a hippie revival. In the last decade, a number of Americans have moved away from society and onto self-sustaining communities. In a fascinating article entitled, "Peace, Love and Social Security: Baby Boomers Retire to the Commune," journalist Anna Spinner notes that since year 2000 the number of communes has increased from about 3,000 to 4,000[6]. This figure represents significant growth. Spinner also writes, of how old hippies from the 1960's and 70's are joining young hippies in the flight from mainstream society to the commune. She attributes the growth of these communes to economic hardship in the wake of the 2008 financial crash. On a final note, Spinner says that many people seem to be seeking to add meaning to their lives, which is something that living in a community can offer.

Many of these new communes are self-fashioned spiritual communities. This means that its members try to inject hippie principles into their day to day lives. Toward these ends, most communes exchange ultra- competitive and capitalist models for cooperative-economic enterprises. Some of these communes have also chosen to implement inclusive and decentralized systems for resolving conflicts and arriving at consensus. These features are seen as preferable to the dominant and corrupt system of politics that currently prevail.

Sustainability

Evidence of the hippie revival can also be seen in the resurrection of old ways of relating to the natural world. The young hippies of today have tried to pick up where their predecessors left off. Some of the following initiatives have been advanced by hippie-minded folk:

---

6 Anna Spinner, "Peace, Love and Social Security: Baby Boomers Retire to the Commune. Atlantic Magazine, November, 21, 2011.

* Education campaigns to inform the public about the harmful effects of nuclear power
* Promotion of clean alternative energy sources such as solar, wind, and hydro power
* Providing instruction for "green" sustainable housing and home construction
* Establishing community gardens in heavy populated urban areas

Intellectuals, who are sympathetic to the hippie mindset, have also been busy re-fashioning the philosophical vision of sustainability to meet the needs of 21st century challenges. For example, Daniel Quinn's book, Ishmael (1995), has enjoyed resurgence as of late. Today, the book is commonly assigned in both high school humanities classes and college courses. A brief description (below) of the book captures this outlook of increased awareness in protecting Mother Nature:

Ishmael is an eco-spiritual classic that revolves around a sage (who is a gorilla) and a middle aged man (the student). Ishmael walks his student through the two philosophical visions guiding mankind's relationship to the natural world. The first vision is that of the "Takers". As the name implies, it is a reference to Western Culture's encroachments upon nature. Ishmael instructs his student that the perspective of the "Takers" condones man's exploitation of the natural world.

In contrast to the "vision" of the "Takers" is that of the "Leavers." The "Leavers" represent the original and long traveled road of human existence. They include much of the world's Indigenous populations who live in communion with nature. Unlike the dominant "Taker" culture, the "Leavers" see the natural world as something to honor, worship, and care after. Quinn then goes on to dissect the philosophical origins, assumptions, and the impacts of the "Taker" philosophy on the planet. The main themes in the book include: the cross-examination of the meaning behind "progress", the negative impact of consumer culture on the world's ecosystems, and the question of our future relationship with the natural world.

Other ecological teachers, like Joan Roelofs, a retired professor from Keene State College in Keene, New Hampshire, have written extensively on the subject of sustainability. In her book, <u>Greening Cities,</u> Roelofs lays out practical ideas for establishing just and sustainable communities. The book is a compilation from her 20 years of research working with towns, environmental activist groups, and various ecological villages. In her work, she hits on such pertinent themes as urban design, democracy and culture, energy, water, transportation, and recreation. This book is now commonly used in university curriculums across the nation.

The Growth of Holistic Health

Hippies have also been active promoters for the virtues of natural medicine. They argue that more holistic remedies provide a direct link between the mind, body, and spirit. Accordingly, an increased emphasis is now being placed on the use of natural herbs for healing. They are seen as both a healthier and cost-effective alternative to the poisonous medications produced by Big Pharma. The rapid growth of natural health food stores nationwide (where herbs and natural remedies are readily purchased) confirms their now popular use.

Hippies have also been active promoters of local, organic farming. For one, this is seen as a healthier and more humane alternative to large-scale commercial farming. The practice also enlists community support for the growth of local farms and farmers. The public's interest in local, organic farming has peaked to such an extent that slogans like "Support your Local Farms" and "No Farms, No Food" often appear on car bumper stickers.

Also, alternative healing techniques such as yoga, hypnotherapy, and Reiki have also been advocated for by hippies. Evidence abounds that each of these practices are beginning to be accepted by the general public. Yoga studios, for example, are a fixture in most cities throughout the country. The practice has caught on like wild fire with the public. In a 2012 survey, Yoga Magazine found that the number of Americans who say they practice has risen 29 % from a number of 15.8 million Americans in 2008 to 20.4 million today.

Hypnosis has also enjoyed a recent wave in popularity. While the practice has long been known in popular culture for its entertainment value, hypnosis has begun to receive attention for its medicinal effects. Hypnotists, like Sandy Lenz, use the practice to help people address some of the following mental health troubles: nicotine addiction, weight loss, anxiety, and various phobias. Significantly, many hypnotists are actively working with returning military veterans afflicted with Post Traumatic Stress Disorder (PTSD).

The practice of Reiki, too, is now gaining popularity. This ancient vehicle aims at healing the body through power of the mind. Variations of this technique have long been practiced by Indigenous peoples the world over (the original energy healers), and was surely mastered by the likes of Jesus Christ when he (reportedly) performed miraculous healings on the sick. Reiki's positive results have been so dramatic that even some hospitals have introduced it into their health regiments. Today, it is not uncommon to find Reiki "masters" spread throughout the land.

The Meditation Revolution

Further evidence of the hippie revival is also being seen in a renewed emphasis on cultivating inner peace. Drawing upon both eastern and indigenous practices, hippies have been active proponents of meditation. The idea behind it is that "sitting" provides an opportunity to access the various facets of one's soul that are buried in a world of logic. It should come as no surprise then, that people would begin to search for meaning in those practices that restore a sense of connection to the sacred. The restoration of this union has a profound effect on one's happiness. Ultimately, the cultivation of inner peace at the personal level translates to the attainment of world peace on the global one.

Hippie-minded folk have been eager promoters of meditation. In the famous hippie bastion of San Francisco, California, they have played a significant role in introducing meditation to several of the city's public schools. One of them, Visitacion Valley Middle School, saw remarkable improvements among its predominantly urban student population after introducing the practice. In the years prior, the school was best known for its high suspension rates, poor test scores, and violence. In fact, it had one of the highest crime rates in the city.

After introducing "quiet time," as the school called it to avoid controversy from skeptical parents, Visitacion Valley saw great improvements. Students recorded some of the lowest suspension rates, highest test scores, and lowest incidents of crime in San Francisco[7]. It should also be of note that the current interest in meditation coincides with several recent studies that link the practice to physical health benefits as well. In one study for example, researchers at Wake Forest University found that 20 minutes of meditation daily decreased pain in chronic sufferers by up to 57 percent[8]. The results from this study have major implications for the future of natural medicine.

The promotion of meditation practice is not only confined to hippie meccas like San Francisco. Meditation centers have popped up across the nation in droves. National societies like "Against the Stream", is one such example. The center's various chapters (located in some major US cities) apply the practice to those who suffer most. They emphasize programs like refuge recovery while still extending the practice to everyone.

The Hippie Revival in Music

Signs of the hippie revival are also being heard in that great vehicle of social change that so galvanized the culture of the 1960s. Genres of music that are traditionally associated with hippies have grown in popularity over the past decade. Reggae music (which is centered on such hippie values as peace, unity, and love) has undergone something of resurgence in the United States[9]. Whole communities of people, centered on reggae, have sprouted up in places not previously receptive to the genre like in Nashville, Tennessee.

---

7 David Kirp. "Meditation Transforms Roughest San Francisco Schools." San Francisco Gate. January, 12, 2014.

8 Sarah Berry. "For Pain Relief, Meditation Better than Drugs." Sydney Morning Herald. February, 20, 2012.

9 Though outside the United States it is the most popular genre globally.

In that city, a small but growing community of people has sprouted up around a couple up and coming Reggae acts. I asked some of the members of this community one question: what values do you think the reggae bands communicate? All answered that positivity, love, and unity were the unifying themes. Reggae music is far from the only genre that communicates hippie values. Blue grass, folk, country, jazz, Blues, Soul, and Native American music serve as equal expressions of Oneness.

MARIJUANA REFORM AND ITS IMPACT ON THE HIPPIE REVIVAL

The recent wave of national marijuana reforms is another indication of the hippie revival. Marijuana has long held a special place within hippie culture for its far reaching benefits for the soul. The key property in Marijuana, THC, has long been associated with the expansion of and connection to one's natural senses. Accordingly, marijuana has also been linked to a heightened self-awareness of both one's internal and external worlds. It should come as no surprise, that marijuana is associated with self-reflection, creativity, and personal insight. It is easy to see why the hippies have embraced a plant that has long been revered by cultures worldwide. A small sampling of such peoples include: the Sadhus of India, the Tantrics of Tibet, the Rastas of Jamaica, and many of the tribes of South Central Africa where "ganja" is symbolic of peace and friendship[10].

Following in the footsteps of our ancestors, hippies have played an important role in pointing out the beneficial effects of this much maligned plant. In so doing, they have taken an active role in the national campaign to reform current marijuana laws. The most notable examples are the legalization of recreational Cannabis in Colorado, Oregon, Washington, and Alaska. It is even legal to grow up to 6 plants in the District of Columbia! This irony should be lost on no one. Notably, in some of these instances, the people themselves (through ballot initiative) dealt the decisive blow to the grave injustices that were. Through its active involvement with

---

10 San Francisco Patient and Resource Center. "Healing and Spiritual Traditions that Use Cannabis."

longtime organizations like the National Organization for the Reform of Marijuana Laws (NORML), it would appear that it is only a matter of time before the hippie is free to smoke this holy sacrament.

The Hippie Revival in Libertarian-Anarchism

The population's growing interest in the political thought of libertarian-anarchism[11] is also an indication of the Hippie Revival. It could be argued that contemporary hippies have injected this movement with much needed energy. Likewise, libertarian-anarchists have provided the hippies with an ideologically sound political base from which to critique the immorality of the American State. The parallels between the hippies and the political thought of libertarian-anarchism are striking. In an article titled "the Hippie Revival in Libertarianism," Monica Lucas writes of the almost natural relationship between the two groups. She suggests that the presence of Hippies is helping drive the movement against an oppressive and violent political establishment[12]. Lucas cites five parallels between the ideals of the two overlapping groups:

- Both groups stand against war
- Both believe in the principle of "Live and Let Live"
- Both place an emphasis on voluntary action
- Both oppose authoritarian models of governance
- Both believe in the principle of Revolution and have great faith that a small minority can reshape the nation's moral fabric through example

The following are just a few brief elaborations upon each correlation.

---

11 Aaron Blake, "22 % of Americans Lean Libertarian." The Washington Post. 10/29/2013.
12 Monica Lucas. "The Hippie Revival in Libertarianism." Students for Liberty forum. July, 30, 2012.

Opposition to War

One of the core hippie values is the emphasis on peace. War would seem an obvious contradiction to these principles. Not surprisingly, hippies have long been active in the anti-war movement. Their opposition to the Vietnam War is a profound and historical case in point. Today, too, hippies have been fervent opponents of each of the US Government's brutal wars in Iraq and Afghanistan. They have also been active opponents of the equally heinous acts committed by Uncle Sam in Pakistan, Libya, and Syria. At a September, 2013 anti-war rally in Nashville, TN, (held in opposition to the Syria intervention) I spoke with many self-described hippies who voiced their unwavering support for the ideas of the then (libertarian minded) presidential candidate Ron Paul.

Live and Let Live

The hippies and libertarian-anarchists also find common ground on the issue of respect for one's personal lifestyle choices and habits. Hippies celebrate the right of freedom of expression. Libertarian-anarchists do too. If one wishes to smoke ganja or marry someone of the same sex, so be it. As long as one does not intrude on the rights of any other, the state has no right to regulate one's behavior. Accordingly, hippies have long been advocates for personal freedom. They have consistently opposed the US Government's War on Drugs, pushed for the protection of the rights of gay couples, and been outspoken supporters of the First Amendment.

Voluntarism

Both Hippies and libertarian-anarchists also share a commitment to the principle of voluntarism. Voluntarism refers to the right for people to freely associate and establish their own models of human interaction. Two such modes of independent action include: establishing alternative systems of economic exchange and adopting participatory conflict resolution models (direct democracy). The culmination of hippie voluntarism in action is the commune (see above). The Libertarian-anarchists, too, believe that all individuals have the right to peacefully dictate their own lifestyle choices, methods of economic exchange, and to adopt their own conflict resolution models. In fact, they devote much of their time contesting the Government's frequent intrusion into these areas.

Opposition to Authoritarian Models of Governance

The parallels between hippies and libertarian-anarchists on this issue are readily apparent. As staunch opponents of societal power structures (church, state, capitalism) it should come as no surprise that hippies have long joined the libertarians in their resistance to the political establishment. Indeed, both groups have stood in fervent opposition to the rise of the American Police State. Not only have Hippies protested the US Government's Domestic wiretapping program, but they have also been steadfast in their opposition of other authoritarian projects such as: indefinite detention, the militarization of America's police forces, and internet censorship.

Belief in the Ability of a Minority to Introduce Change

Libertarian-anarchists have been vocal agents of change. They maintain that ordinary Americans have the capacity to reign in and disarm the authoritarian powers of the modern American Government. Their belief in the power of a minority to reshape the political and economic landscapes is easily translated to the hippie. Though hippies constitute a minority, they have nonetheless been quite resilient in their belief that they can help expand the collective consciousness of the planet.

The global phenomenon known as "Occupy" is a good example of this vision put into action. The Occupy protests of 2011 were heavily infused with the spirit of young hippies, before eventually spreading to most major cities throughout the country. The protests, which erupted in the aftermath of the 2008 US Government bailout of major Wall Street banks, were a response to the intertwined issues of corporate greed and government corruption. "Occupiers", as they came to be called, built encampments or mini tent societies in the public parks of major cities. Within these communities protesters created signs and pamphlets to share with the general public, established food kitchens to feed the activists, constructed their own volunteer medic staffs, put together a gift economy of exchange, and conducted teach ins on everything from meditation to the history of protest movements in the United States. According to David Garber, an activist-writer, the hippie influenced Occupy movement offered a glimpse into what a moral, post-revolutionary society might look like.

SOME FINAL THOUGHTS

There are three main ideas I wish to leave the reader with: first, I want you to know that there is a new-found interest in hippie culture and beliefs. Second, that one should find great hope in the future of both humanity and the planet. In spite of the greed, deception, and hatred that permeates much of our society, there are also deep pockets of love forming simultaneously. The hippie revival is proof that mankind is about to take a giant leap forward into the way of spirit consciousness. Finally, I hope readers will be inspired to add their own contributions to those facets of the hippie revival that I may have overlooked. This writing is only an inception point for conversation on an emerging phenomenon. After all, we will only come to comprehend the full scale and impact of this moment of becoming through the constant sharing of our diverse experiences and perspectives.

The Hippie Lexicon

(The terms presented here are not meant to be all encompassing. If you have a righteous definition or term to add send it to the website: www.forrestrivers.com with your name!)

BABYION: 1) A TERM USED to refer to a society devoid of spirit and in pursuit of ego. 2) A model of social organization that extols profit through the exploitation of the people. 3) Commercial society. 4) Meaning essentially the same thing as "the man." 5) Term has been popularized by followers of the Rasta Faith.

Being: 1) Spirit. 2) Existence. 3) A miracle.

Capitalism: 1) An economic system by which the few profit off the many. 2) The unholy alliance between government and corporations designed to maximize profits. 3) Exploitation by other name.

Car: 1) A sophisticated rolling chunk of metal and plastic that takes us to our desired destinations. 2) An instrument originally created to facilitate commerce. 3) A piece of machinery that keeps us looking busy.

Cell phone: 1) A technological device designed to facilitate communication. 2) A hand held instrument that serves to further alienate us from self and others. 3) A hazard for drivers everywhere. 4) A distraction from the present moment.

City: 1) Originally a meeting point for the local exchange of goods, services, ideas, and culture. 2) The backdrop for shameless displays of wealth acquisition and power. 3) A corporation that pretends it is serving the public interest. 4) That which perpetuates moral corruption.

Commune: 1) A community of people who share a common vision, interest, property, and resources. 2) A mode of living inspired by tribal societies. 3) Cooperative-group living. 4) An alternative to authoritarian Government.

Community: 1) A group of individuals who engage in harmonious being amongst themselves and with the earth. 2) Sustained acts of reciprocity between groups of people. 3) Belonging. 4) Love.

Consumerism: 1) The ideology that emphasizes the unlimited acquisition of worldly possessions. 2) A mindset derived from unbridled greed and competition and resulting in the unsustainable extraction of Earth's resources. 3) The engine driving capitalism. 4) That which both Jesus and Buddha decried.

Corporation: 1) A profit-making institution that shields the wealthy from liability. 2) A psychopathic organization replete with the rights and freedoms of actual living and breathing persons. 3) An entity that plunders another's resources for profit, gain, and power. 4) That which stifles authentic human interaction. 5) Absurdity in action.

Democracy: 1) A system in which the people play an active and direct role in the resolution of their own social disputes and problems. 2) A type of conflict resolution model by which the decisions affecting day to day life are rendered directly by the people. 3) Rule by the many. 4) That which, despite its claims to be, the United States is not. 5) An illusion for much of the world's population.

Education: 1) Originally conceived by the ancients as a pathway to inner growth and personal freedom. 2) A modern scheme of social conditioning masquerading as truth. 3) Another great source of profit for the rich and powerful.

Ego: 1) The false worship of self. 2)That which runs counter to spirit.

Energy: 1) Vibrations of the spirit that are found in all beings. 2) One's Chi. 3) Life force.

Environment: 1) One's total realm of activity comprised of both voluntary and involuntary interactions. 2) The source that molds one's conception of reality. 3) Place of being. 4) The natural world.

Expression: 1) Any act that is inspired by one's connection to spirit. 2) The soul's vehicle of communication. 3) Creativity.

Farmers Market: 1) A place where people gather to support the local farmers in their community. 2) A marketplace where one finds nutritious food for the mind, body, and spirit. 3) The counter to the devil itself (Monsanto). 4) Community.

Freedom: 1) A condition by which one is at liberty to pursue any paths pursuant to their spiritual journey. 2) A state of mind that emphasizes detachment from worldly concerns and possessions. 3) Also implies mutual respect for all beings' personal choices and paths. 4) Nature.

Friendship: 1) The gift of repeated acts of compassion between two people. 2) Participation in one's moments of joy and suffering.

Gifting: 1) An act of reciprocity by which one gives away something of value to another without expecting anything in return. 2) An act of giving detached from ego.

Government: 1) The systematic organization of violence designed to protect the rich and powerful from the meek. 2) A violent entity that has been responsible for some of mankind's most heinous crimes and atrocities. 3) An institution which works to keep all of God's people divided. 4) An organization that earns its wealth from the stolen labors of others.

Hippie: 1) A person who tries to attain personal liberation through practicing the values of soulful expression, peace, charity, independence, and reverence for the Earth through love. 2) An eternal child of love.

Humility: 1) The recognition that no person is better nor worse than any other. 2) An understanding that we are all one. 3) The ability to see that God is in everyone.

Internet: 1) A network of information and knowledge that has great potential to inform, share, and organize. 2) A technological innovation commonly harnessed toward narcissistic ends (I.E. Facebook).

Karma: 1) Energy vibrations resulting from one's thoughts, intentions, and actions. 2) A divine law of the universe. 3) That which encourages awareness. 4) Proof of Oneness.

Kindred Spirit: 1) The unification of two eternal souls. 2) Soul mates. 3) A reminder of love. 4) A spiritual companion.

Love: 1) Awareness that God is in everything and everyone. 2) The essence of being. 3) The Divine Power. 4) Communion with spirit.

Making Love: 1) A divine expression shared between two souls. 2) The coming together of two kindred spirits. 3) An act of creation. 4) Love.

Marijuana: 1) A mystical herb closely associated with spirit. 2) A green plant known for its tremendous healing properties. 3) Something that is just about perfect for all occasions... such as music shows, hiking, and prayer/meditation. 4) That which unites.

Medicine: 1) A practice originally conceived of by shamans in which natural herbs from the planet, as well as energy harnessed from the universe, were used to heal the sick and weary. 2) An organized system of mass deception whereby greedy corporations profit off of peoples' illness. 3) A modern day predicament for mankind in which doctors are not trained to heal.

Meditation: 1) The process by which one unlocks the key to their inner self. 2) The art of focused contemplation. 3) The turning of one's attention inwards. 4) The silencing of the ego. 5) Mindfulness. 6) Stillness.

Money: 1) Man's arbitrary assigning of value to things that can't be defined. 2) The thing that perpetuates human misery and suffering. 3) That which corrupts the human spirit. 4) The inception point of greed. 5) An expression of ego. 6) That which reverts adults back to children.

Native(s): 1) Original inhabitants. 2) Tribal people who live in harmony with nature. 3) Deeply spiritual beings. 4) Those who have advanced the progress of the human race. 5) Our ancestors.

Nature: 1) The green oasis from which we all came from and to where we will return to. 2) Our natural state. 3) An antidote to ego. 4) The environment. 5) Freedom. 6) A humble teacher. 7) A mirror upon one's self. 8) God. 9) A community of all beings.

Oneness: 1) A perpetual state of peace 2) The realization that all beings are interconnected 3) A state of bliss that transcends common notions of space and time. 4) An outlook that regards all of creation as sacred and as one. 5) Reality.

Organized Religion: 1) The perversion of the spiritual teachings of Jesus, Mohammad, Buddha, and Krishna by aspirants for power and control. 2) A foundation built on fear through the submission of one's soul to authority. 3) An institution which has (in conjunction with Government) carried out heinous crimes against both man and nature. 4) A great illusion for spiritual seekers.

Peace: 1) A state of love. 2) The embrace of stillness. 3) Heaven. 4) Nirvana.

Plane: 1) A flying object that demonstrates our mastery over the sky. 2) A great display of human ego.

Police: 1) An armed machinery of violence in the service of Government. 2) A repressive organization who achieves social control through coercion and violence. 3) The Teeth for the Government's unjust laws and decrees. 4) Thugs with badges. 5) Severely damaged souls in need of healing and love.

Progress: 1) A belief system that justifies the exploitation of nature for the convenience of mankind. 2) An excuse for mankind's ravaging of the natural world. 3) An intellectual framework that promotes consumerism. 4) Propaganda that extols the submission of the natural world to the human drives of ego. 5) The subordination of the human spirit to that of ego.

Reggae: 1) A musical and cultural tradition born of a combination of older popular styles and folk music from the hilly countryside of Jamaica. 2) A deep tradition of spiritually inspired music. 3) Seeking Jah and striving for unity among all things. 4) That which deals with love, a yearning for a more natural environment, and the nature of living in a violent culture. 5) Positivity.

Science: 1) A realm of research and discovery originally devoted to questions of our origins, evolution, and reality. 2) A super structure in the service of the rich and powerful. 3) Something that has severed its connection from spirit. 4) A man made discipline elevated to God like status by ironic Atheists.

Shrooms: 1) Slang for a particular type of hallucinogenic mushroom. 2) A mushroom known for inducing great spiritual visions and insights. 3) A shaman's rite of passage.

Spirit: 1) The essence of self. 2) Being. 3) That which ego is not.

Spirituality: 1) A journey to inner knowing. 2) A search for the divine within. 3) One's chosen medium(s) of connecting to God.

Sustainability: 1) A perspective that holds deep reverence for Mother Earth. 2) Taking only what you need from the planet. 3) The vision carried out by most Indigenous cultures. 4) An idea that both governments and corporations trumpet but rarely follow.

Tree Hugger: 1) Meaning literally one who hugs trees. 2) A person who embraces a tree. 3) A disparaging term used by the dominant culture to refer to earth activists.

Unity: 1) A collective awareness that we are all children of god. 2) A prerequisite to the achievement of peace. 3) The breaking down of all forms of classification between man, and between man and other beings.

Universe: 1) The intricate web of creation. 2) Allness. 3) The unity of God. 4) The Source. 5) The Cosmos.

Yoga: 1) The movement of spirit energy to balance one's being. 2. A practice in present time awareness. 3) A Reconnection with source. 4) A form of meditation. 5. Namaste!

*Thank you to Rose, Sean M, Alex C, and Alec N for their contributions to the Hippie Lexicon.

Psychedelic Encounters
with Spirit

"In San Francisco, when heavy psychedelics were at
their peak, people were seeing things three or four
times a week that one sight of it should have gone
wham and just straightened them. They should have
said 'wow look at that; and just got cool right then, but
they were so jaded from having done it a hundred times
that it didn't have any juice. As familiar as religious
experience may become to us, we don't dare let it get
ordinary. This is called keeping sacred things sacred."

-STEPHEN GASKIN

AFTER MANY YEARS, I THINK I now fully understand the hippies' preoc-
cupation with psychedelics in the 1960's and 70's. If they are taken with
right intent, psychedelics provide an incredible pathway into the spiritual
realm. In the first year of my own awakening, I enjoyed three (inspiring)
psychedelic encounters with spirit. Each trip revealed profound insights
into my being and addressed the following age old questions about life:

* What is the nature of our reality?
* Why are we here?

* What is my life's purpose and how do I attain it?
* What is the nature of God and where can IT be found?

In addition to providing insights into these questions, each encounter with psychedelics also unveiled messages about my own journey. In my attempts to decipher its meanings, a type of divine communication was opened between my soul and the Universe. In each of the three trips, I also noticed that the person who supplied the psychedelics played a pivotal role in relating the respective life messages. Though not always direct participants in my encounters, the suppliers were crucial actors in each of the journeys. Finally, I also felt that the set and setting (the nature of the environment and the person I tripped with) amplified the quality of each of these experiences. What follows is a detailed account of three psyche-delic encounters and how they impacted my own spiritual growth. These key points are described in detail:

* The central theme or message that was conveyed in each trip
* The significance of the person who made the trip possible and how that individual tied into those themes that were conveyed
* How the set and setting influenced the quality of the overall experience
* How lessons from each of the three trips came to form one uni-versal truth

Journey One: A Spirit Dance with DMT

During my time as a college professor, I have encountered some of the most interesting and eccentric of students, but no one quite like Cameron. Though he was only 20 years old, Cameron was wise beyond his years. I first met him when he was a campus reporter for the student-run maga-zine. One day, he came to my office to interview me for an article he was writing entitled "Outlawed Imagination: A Psychedelic Look into the Assault on Religious Freedoms." He had (in his own words) heard about the new "hippie government professor" on campus, and wanted to gather my insights on a fascinating topic.

He asked me the following question: did I think that the use of psychedelics for spiritual use should be protected by the First Amendment of the United States Constitution? I answered that I thought it should. I said that the US Government targeted psychedelic users in order to maintain control over the American people. My reasoning was that psychedelics have the effect of detaching our minds from societal conditioning. So why, during the course of a trip, wouldn't one begin to question a structure built solely upon deceit and violence? Cameron liked my response, and the two of us ended up talking for about an hour. We discussed a great deal about ganja, meditation, and our own college's suppression of speech. Finally, our own past encounters with psychedelics came up in conversation. I mentioned to him that I had used them recreationally a handful of times in the past. Cameron looked at me perplexed, and the following dialogue (pieced together with his permission) ensued:

Cameron: What do you mean you used them recreationally?
Me: I don't know. I guess I used them because I thought they would be fun. I mean mushrooms just seemed really interesting to try.
Cameron: Well you know, psychedelics have a much more important purpose than to be used for recreation. They were put here by God to help us along our spiritual journey. They are meant to help us grasp the meaning of existence.
Me: (laughing) is that why you are openly advocating for their use in this article?
Cameron: Yes (laughs). With so much hate in the world coming from our unchecked egos we have severed ourselves from spirit. Psychedelics help us reconnect to it.

The following fall, Cameron enrolled in my American Government course to continue his formal education. In turn, I pursued my informal education with him on the topic of psychedelics. During the semester,

Cameron introduced me to the likes of Graham Hancock, a historian of shamanism (who I ended up weaving into my class), and Rick Strassman, a medical doctor who became known for his research on DMT. As the semester drew to a close, Cameron invited me to join him on a DMT trip. I eagerly accepted and the two of us set up a time to meet at my apartment. One afternoon, Cameron came over with his pipe in hand. We exchanged greetings and then he gave me some brief instructions/ background about DMT:

- DMT was to be smoked not ingested as is commonly done with other naturally occurring psychedelics such as mushrooms and peyote.
- DMT would produce both visual images (hallucinations) and a strong connection with the inner self. He added that the hallucinations would come in a series of waves. That is, I would fall in and out of the hallucinogenic state.
- I could expect to lose my sense of time. While the trip would only last somewhere in the vicinity of 35-40 minutes, it would feel much longer. Maybe even several hours. Cameron termed this effect "spirit time".

Following his brief instructions, we sat back in my apartment and began to prepare for our departure into the spirit world. In preparation, I chose a highly meditative setting for this event. I turned off the lights, flipped on my two orange salt lamps, lit incense in the room, put on some meditation music by the composer Karunesh, and packed a fresh bowl of ganja to smoke. Finally, I placed two pillows down on the floor for each of us.

Cameron packed the DMT pipe full of a white powdery substance and took the first hit. He then passed it to me. I ripped a small pull off of the sacred piece; and almost immediately I was overcome by a euphoric feeling. I began to feel weightless as I picked up on those subtle aspects of being that go mostly unnoticed during traditional states of consciousness. I became aware of the energy vibrations of my room-mate's dog Bliss. As soon as we took our first hits, she walked across the room and sat right down between the two of us. This was abnormal behavior for her. Usually she was a bit more cautious around strangers. Then it dawned on me, Bliss was attracted to the energy in the room. Cameron picked up on her vibrations, too. He whispered to me that she was a very old soul.

Following our encounter with my roommate's dog, I tuned into the rhythm of my own breathing. This sense of awareness eclipsed anything I had experienced in my regular meditations. I focused my attention back on Cameron, and he nodded, so we pulled a second hit off the pipe. I laid back on the floor and fell into a deep meditation. During this "time", two spectacular visions occurred.

The First DMT Vision: A Ring of Love

Deep in my meditation, I arrived at a place where I saw one large ring of people standing in puffy white clouds. The people were all smiling, laughing, and embracing one another. At first, I couldn't make out their faces. However, I felt as though I knew each person. As I walked over toward the ring, I began to make out the faces. I saw immediate family, current best friends, and my dog Abbie. I also saw three ex-girlfriends and my two closest friends from college. Going back further in time, I was astonished to find that my best friends from high school and childhood were there as well.

Remarkably, the ring also included people with whom I had endured falling outs with. For example, another ex-girlfriend stood in the ring smiling, as did my best friend from high school. He stood in the middle of the ring and extended his hand out to mine when I approached him. We then pulled each other in close for a hug. I took my place in the ring and we all held hands and began to spin together in a circle. This was a dance of peace and harmony. The scene rushed over me with such positive vibrations, that I felt waves of tears streaming down my face.

When I came out of the meditation, I began to piece together the deeper meaning of this vision. I came to a simple interpretation: life's essence is love. We are here to perfect its expression in human form. From this vision, I also gathered that love is unconditional. It doesn't acknowledge tensions between close friends or loved ones. Rather, if a person touched your heart at any point in time, one's love will always prevail. Love is eternal, as it transcends both time and space. It also became clear that love knows nothing of separateness; only of oneness. I thought of how the former emanates from the ego, and the latter from the depths of the soul. I also pondered the likelihood that separateness arises from the ego's tendency to judge, label, and assign arbitrary values to being. This, I also concluded, was the opposite case with our souls. True spirit sees all creation as one whole.

Cameron came out of his own meditation only moments after mine. To my amazement, the first words out of his mouth were: "love is at the root of everything". To which I responded, "It really is". We both just smiled and nodded. It was as if we were having the same vision. Cameron repacked the pipe and we partook in the last of 3 hits. I fell into a second meditation that expanded my insights of love.

The Spirit Molecule and the Out of Body Experience

In this second meditation, I experienced something that I had only read and heard about before...an out of body experience. This phenomenon occurs when the soul (the spirit consciousness) detaches itself from the physical body and wonders about freely. This experience is also sometimes referred to as "astral travel". In the moments leading up to my out of body experience, I felt intense waves of love (forgiveness, acceptance, gratitude, and joy) rush throughout my body. Three images seemed to trigger these feelings. The first was of the poetic mesh of joy and suffering I felt in the wake of a recent break-up. The second image was of my dog Abbie and I on a long walk through the woods. This vision conjured up great feelings of peace and serenity. Finally, I thought of all those people in my life who provided me with unconditional love and support. As the emotions of love overtook my body, I felt my hands and feet go numb. My arms and legs followed. Then my body began to tingle. The vibrations felt like great currents of energy flowing through me. My chest then grew tight as a gentle calm fell over me. I was weightless.

What happened next will sound unbelievable to would be skeptics: my soul took flight into the sky. I recall thinking that this is what it feels like to be a bird. My essence flew over a lake, soared over the trees, and high above the mountain tops. I experienced a total state of oneness. I felt a sense of liberation that is difficult to put into words. In the days following this encounter, I tried to convey it through poetry:

"Outer Realm"
Lifting
Ever higher
Above the trees
And past the mountains
Soft clouds direct me toward
A beautiful world of higher knowing
Shifting and turning a celebration of life
Reading my bearings in the blue majestic sky

An awe inspiring love the source of this experience

My descent from the source of oneness begins
Through the wise and fluffy white clouds
Past the tall and glorious mountains
Below the elegant green trees
Humbled by this encounter
Preparation for arrival
Slowly lowering
Returning

The phenomenon of the out of body experience is actually not as shocking as it sounds. It is facilitated by the same substance (DMT) that is present in our bodies when we sleep. A tiny pine cone like structure called the pineal gland (coined the "third eye" by spiritual mystics), produces the compound. More astounding to me, was the power of love. If DMT served as a catalyst for this experience, then love served as the conveyor between the soul and its ultimate liberation. This explains why in "Outer Realm," I placed the words, "an awe inspiring love the source of this experience", at the center of the two wings in flight.

The out of body experience shed light on the question of how we should interpret reality. In the world of western reductionist science, everything is boiled down to terms of physical matter. In the words of Graham Hancock, the west maintains that we "are all just meat". Thus, when the body dies, "reality" as we know it comes to an end. Neuro scientists, however, have been **unable** to rule out the possibility that human consciousness exists separate from the mind. If (as many indigenous cultures hold) consciousness is the soul's awareness, then we are all much more than "just meat".

Following my astral journey, I am convinced that there are separate spiritual realms of existence. At the moment, such a conception of reality is beyond our society's comprehension. If there are "alternate "dimensions that comprise the totality of what we call "reality", this raises some obvious questions:

- How many spirit worlds or dimensions are there?
- Are these spirit worlds or dimensions the places our souls go when the physical body dies?
- Why do humans place such a disproportionate emphasis on the physical form?
- What are the implications of astral travel for reincarnation?
- Does time as we know it even exist in the spiritual realms? If not, what does that mean for our notions of past, present, and future?

I have not the answers to any of these questions. It is unlikely I ever will. This much is clear though: there are planes of existence far beyond what we conceive of in our culture. From the out of body, I came to see that our conception of reality reflects the narrow outlook of one dominant sub-group, the scientific community. What makes their conception of reality any more credible than various mystic sects who believe reality is profoundly spiritual? Such were my first thoughts in the moments after this experience. These insights reinforced the key theme of the trip: life's essence is love.

As the DMT started wearing off, Cameron and I both sat up and began to share our insights and visions. Incredibly, we came away with almost identical interpretations of reality. Over a bowl of ganja, the two of us continued to discuss our experiences. Finally, Cameron stood up and announced that he had to leave. I sprang to my feet and hugged him. He invited me for a future "dance" with DMT. I readily accepted. After Cameron's departure, I reflected back on his comments from a year earlier:

> "With so much hate in the world coming from our unchecked egos---we have severed ourselves from spirit. Psychedelics help us reconnect to it."

Remarkable I thought, God sends down messengers at just the right point in one's journey. Undeniably, Cameron was one of those messengers.

Trip 2: Soul Healing On Magic Mushrooms

My second encounter with psychedelics took place about 6 weeks after the DMT trip. This journey, too, would come to impact my spiritual growth. The key themes of this trip built upon those from my first "spirit dance". Four months removed from a nearly 3-year long relationship with an ex-girlfriend, I had been working through the conflicted range of emotions that accompanies a break-up: liberation, sadness, nostalgia, and hope. I tried to capture them in a poem I wrote a few weeks after the event.

"Four Directions"
The Compass spins in four directions
North, South, East, and West
The north points toward my soul's liberation
The south shepherds it into the nostalgic abyss
The east unveils the bitter welt of sadness
The west heralds the dawn of a new consciousness
The needle continues to spin mercilessly
Leaving in its path a world without bearings

Romantically speaking, I had moved well on beyond her. However, I still experienced feelings of regret for my past behavior in the relationship. In the weeks leading up to this journey, the two of us had started reaching out to one another as friends again. One afternoon, this ex-girlfriend called me and said that she had been given magic mushrooms by an acquaintance. She didn't enjoy psychedelics, so she asked if I wanted to purchase them from her. I gave her a resounding yes! I felt bewildered by both the dumb luck of the mushrooms finding me, and by the identity of the supplier. What were the chances I thought? A few days went by and the two of us met outside her apartment to make the transfer, quickly exchanging the mushrooms and money before parting ways.

Upon returning home, I informed my roommate Sean, that I had bought some Psilocybin (the hallucinogenic compound) mushrooms. I told him that he and I would be doing them together. He gave me his customary nod of approval and exclaimed, *"Right on, brother man. You don't have to twist my arm"*. With that, we decided to ingest them in the coming weeks. We left the day and time open to allow for spontaneity. Sean was an obvious choice to journey with for two reasons. First, because he is like an adopted brother. While a brother is usually thought of as being blood-related—which he is not---labels do not apply here.

Second, because he is a deeply intuitive person. A psychedelic encounter is intended to be a dance with spirit. So, it made sense to journey with one who had the same mindset. This is all to say nothing of his own storied past with psychedelics. Sean had enjoyed spectacular visions while on his own trips. He recalled one such occasion while journeying at a music festival. The event was located on an old Indian burial ground. During the trip, he remembers seeing hundreds of Native American spirits rise up from the ground armed with hatchets. The apparitions proceeded to hack at many of the festival goers. He recalls gaining insight into the anger and despair that the tormented spirits were releasing at the time. The attendees were clearly regarded as intruders. The next day, Sean discovered that he had in fact been camping out on an old burial ground. An individual so attuned to energy is one you want to share a psychedelic experience with.

One week later, Sean came home from work late, and I asked him if he would like to go on the mushroom journey. He looked at me surprised and said: *"Its 11 pm, you want to do them now?"* I just nodded my head yes. A moment later, Sean overcame his brief hesitancy and excitedly said, *"OK, brother man. Let's do it!"* As with the DMT trip, setting made all the difference. We hooked up our customary salt lamps, lit incense, dimmed the lights, put on music by Karunesh, and packed up a bowl of ganja. After smoking for fifteen minutes, we divided up the mushrooms to ingest. Because of their foul taste, the eating of mushrooms can be an adventure in and of itself! I put my half of the "shrooms" in a peanut butter sandwich. It wasn't half bad. Like the well-seasoned veteran he was, Sean ate his raw!

Before proceeding with the journey's unfolding, some general background is needed about magic mushrooms. The intensity of a psychedelic trip will vary depending on one's size and weight. The amount that one ingests is also an important factor. For this trip, we both ate ½ of an eighth each. This was more than enough to foster light visions and engender a heightened sense of perception. Our dosage levels, however, would not have come anywhere close to producing the kinds of hallucinations experienced by the late Hunter S. Thompson in his book, <u>Fear and Loathing in Las Vegas.</u>

Depending on the factors above, the duration of a typical mushroom trip lasts anywhere between 4-6 hours. It is significantly longer than DMT, but much shorter than acid - which can last 8-12 hours. Magic

Mushrooms also hits your system more gradually than DMT. Depending on the efficiency of one's metabolism, it can sometimes take up to 45 min-utes-1 hour for the psilocybin to kick in. This lag effect, can sometimes produce mild anxiety in users. This is why, it is wise to select a peaceful environment before ingesting.

As with the use of any psychedelic, one should approach their encoun-ters with the right intent. By "right intent," I mean that one consciously spells out their intentions before partaking. Too many times, users of mushrooms (as with all psychedelics) begin a trip without first acknowl-edging (from within) a deeper reason for doing so. This is especially the case for recreational users. Too often, they perceive their trips as having been negative ordeals. All psychedelic encounters should be honored as a voyage into the spirit world.

Into an Elevator of Light

The magic mushrooms kicked in about 45 minutes after ingestion. Almost immediately, Sean and I fell into deep meditations. In stillness, I encoun-tered an incredible vision. I started to see translucent lights that grew brighter whenever I felt emotive expressions of love. For example, when I experienced the feeling of acceptance the light grew radiant. The feel-ing of forgiveness produced an even greater white light. I would see ever brilliant rays as the inspiration of love blossomed. As the feeling of for-giveness gradually gave way to understanding, I saw awe inspiring lights. There, in Oneness, the sensational vibrations of love overwhelmed my being. Then, as quickly as I rose through the various stages of emotions, I returned back to a place of neither darkness nor light.

The "elevator lights" (as I came to call them) felt as though they were instructing me spiritually. However, maybe I was in control of this whole encounter. Was it possible that the Creator and the God within me were working in tandem through the laws of attraction? These are the inter-nal questions I asked myself in the throes of the mushroom trip. This vision reinforced the key theme from my DMT trip: "life's true essence is love". A new revelation also began to emerge: the higher frequencies of acceptance, forgiveness, and understanding, are crucial expressions of the power of love.

The lasting remnants of this vision laid in the source from which these emotions ran. At the start of the meditation, I began to reflect back on my past relationship. I initially felt guilty. This feeling came with a corresponding dimness in light. I experienced guilt for the lack of respect that I had exhibited in the past. As the stew of guilt boiled, I had flashbacks of each of the many instances in which my actions inflicted great harm upon her and myself. Fortunately, just as suddenly as I had been overtaken by feelings of guilt, a calm wave of compassion splashed over me. The lights grew brighter still, and with tears in my eyes, I silently made amends for my past regrets and finally achieved acceptance. By then, radiant light overwhelmed me. Having acknowledged that my actions were far from perfect in that relationship, I was now working on forgiving myself. The calming lights grew so bright, that I felt like I was swimming in Oneness. It wasn't clear if *IT* was outside or inside of me. To be sure, I felt the presence of a great creator, though I knew it had no form. It felt more like a great ball of energy. An intense knowing came over me, and insights as to why she and I had crossed paths in the first place came easily to me now. It also dawned on me that she had been placed in my path for a reason too.

From this trip, I also felt that I gained a greater understanding into the nature of God. Deep in meditation, the Infinite felt like a gentle energy. Far from a being who judges and condemns, *IT* felt like the essence of unconditional love. The "elevator lights", also seemed to confirm the importance of addressing our own suffering. As the Buddha pointed out, becoming aware that we suffer is the easy part. More challenging, is letting go of those attachments that feed our suffering. That is why the Buddha placed so much emphasis on the teachings of self- liberation. We are our own paths back to oneness.

After a long while (two hours perhaps) spent in mediation, Sean and I emerged only moments apart. How strange, I thought, that it had happened with Cameron the same way. Is it possible that the energy fields of all participants bind as one during a psychedelic trip? We discussed this possibility and shared our insights with one another. It is interesting to note that Sean had very similar takeaways from his own trip. He had also been in a recent breakup (with a partner of 13 years) and had experienced similar insights about forgiveness, acceptance, and understanding. After some great discussion, the two of us experienced a brief period (maybe 30-45 minutes) when we fell in and back out of mediation. Finally, after repeating this pattern, we reached a point where we both simply nodded at each other and retreated to our respective rooms to reflect some more and journal.

In their own right, each of the three journeys were forms of soul healing. This journey felt especially so. Since this experience, I have become more aware of my own unhealthy attachments and of the need to let go of past suffering. Valuable lessons that all of us could learn.

Trip 3: A Spirit Journey on Mushroom Tea

The camping trip began with great anticipation. After a two-hour drive along twisting and winding roads we finally arrived at our destination. For the next 72 hours, Fall Creek Falls State Park was to be our home. My kindred spirit, Rose, had visited the park several times as a child. She said it had spectacular hiking trails and breathtaking waterfall views. Due to the nausea filled car ride, we were both a bit tense and wanted to get into nature immediately. With only two hours of sunlight remaining, we chose a short 3-mile hike that would have us back before sunset.

Overjoyed at being in nature, we pranced through the woods like two forest ferries on an afternoon stroll. About one half mile into the hike, we crossed paths with a man who appeared to be in his mid to late 20's. He was tall—about 6 feet 3 inches, with short blond hair. The three of us came to the same overlook at a gorgeous waterfall. We exchanged pleasantries and carried on our ways. In that brief interaction, Rose and I could both feel his strong presence. His energy was calm and he seemed genuine. As we parted ways, I turned to Rose and said: "If we see that guy again, we have to make it a point to smoke him up".

I had packed a couple grams of ganja for this occasion, and considered it something of a peace gesture to offer it to other hikers. Only a few months earlier, we were presented with a similar situation. Rose and I were climbing a few peaks at Pisgah National Forest, when we ran into a man atop a mountain. We ended up striking up a conversation and offered to smoke with him. The very next day, we ran into a group of college students who returned the favor. Instant karma! The tradition of smoking others up (especially in the natural world) connotes friendship and reciprocity.

High on both nature and ganja, Rose and I continued along the gorgeous trail for another mile, until something caught our eye. It was the same man who we had run into earlier. Destiny had arranged for our paths to cross once more. I turned to her and just nodded. We approached the man and introduced ourselves. He said that his name was Jonathan and that he was riding on his bicycle from Ann Arbor, Michigan (where he lived) down to Florida to visit his girlfriend. Once there, he would enjoy a brief respite. Then, he would resume his journey up the eastern coast from Florida to Maine. Amazed, I asked him how he was supporting himself on this trip. He explained that he had raised a little money from a small fund raiser with close friends and family. For the most part, though, he was surviving off the good will of strangers. In response, I kept the questions coming:

Me: Where do you stay at night?
Him: I packed a hammock and sleep in the trees.
Me: What places have you visited on your way to Florida?
Him: Major state parks along the way. I hike and then make camp.
Me: Why do you do this?
Him: Bicycling has always been a passion of mine. I get lost in the moment when I bike; solo biking is a soulful experience for me.
Me: Don't you get lonely along the way riding solo?

Him: I never get lonely on the road. For me, it is liberating. I meet a lot of nice people along the way at the various state parks. Additionally, (and he said this with a big grin) I brought along some magic mushrooms for the trip. I mix the mushrooms with tea and honey and spend much of the time riding in reflection.

The three of us continued to walk for about an eighth of a mile together. During this brief stroll, Rose and I came to learn more about this fascinating character. His life philosophy was simple: do with your time what you are passionate about and don't attach yourself to material things. Jonathan explained though, that Dominant Culture emphasizes just the opposite, to devote your time to what will make you money so that you may acquire more consumer rewards. Life was meant to be simple, but humans over complicate things. Jonathan was quite cynical about society, but still expressed an unwavering faith in humanity. From his direct experience, he said that the majority of people want to do good, some just get stuck in the web of social conditioning.

Jonathan then went on to describe the countless acts of generosity that he encountered while on the road. Two such instances included strangers taking him in for the night and a person who returned a lost wallet to him. Jonathan had such a fresh perspective on life. What's more is that he chose to seize upon the opportunity we all have to be free. By this point, I had assumed that Jonathan must have studied philosophy for years. How else, I thought, to explain his almost natural detachment from societal pressures? Before parting ways on the trail, I asked him one final question:

Me: So, you must read and study a lot of spiritual writings?
Him: I don't really read a lot of books because the words of others are not grounded in direct experience. Insights into one's journey should be arrived through one's direct encounters.

On his own terms, Jonathan had clearly arrived at some beautiful insights about life. No gurus necessary. Just a commitment to live life fully in the present, "to be here NOW." This insight would come to form the central theme in my third psychedelic encounter. After this inspired exchange, the three of us walked together in silence for a little while. Finally, Jonathan broke it. He offered to give the two of us a large cup of his mushroom tea concoction. Rose and I both smiled at each other, then back at him, and accepted his offer. We arranged a time and a place for him to meet us with the tea.

Rose and I continued on our hike. When it was over, we walked back to the main campsite where we had parked our car. We waited there for Jonathan. About ten minutes past, before we saw him roll up on his bicycle. He jumped off the bike and we hugged. Within a few moments, Jonathan began to heat the tea up for us on a camp burner. While he did so, I pulled out my bowl and Rose packed it full of ganja. We offered it to our new friend. He readily accepted and told us of a more secluded campsite we could stay at a couple miles down the road. As the bowl entered its second rotation, a park ranger pulled up behind us. Rose shoved the bowl into her pocket. The Ranger informed us that we could not stay at the campsite where our car was parked. He then instructed us to register for a camp site. At that moment, I recall thinking how absurd it was to enforce petty park regulations in nature. Most of us leave the confines of the city to escape from them in the first place. I also chuckled to myself, because unbeknown to the Ranger was a hot brewing cup of mushroom tea right in front of his face!

The Ranger pulled away, and we took out our bowl again and passed it around. Jonathan finished warming the tea and handed us a bottle's worth (1/8 ounce) to split between the two of us. We thanked him and also took his advice on where to camp. He told us that he would stop by in the morning to see how we enjoyed the concoction and to say goodbye, for Jonathan was to set off on the next stage of his journey to Florida. This trek would include a grueling 60 mile ride through the Tennessee Mountains. Staring down at the bottle of mushroom tea, Rose and I deliberated on when would be the best time to drink it. We decided on the following afternoon.

The next morning, we were awakened by the barking of our beloved dog Abbie. Jonathan was standing right outside our tent. As promised, he stopped by to ask how our mushroom trip was and to bid us farewell. We told him that we were partaking that afternoon. He smiled. Jonathan then exchanged his cell phone number with Rose and I. As a show of support, we gave him a few energy bars for his journey. We all embraced and went on our separate ways. For this special occasion, Rose and I had chosen a trail out to a waterfall and back. The path was not as well-known as other trails at the park. We would have privacy on our journey. Taking turns holding the tea, we walked about two miles before finally settling at a comfortable spot in the woods a bit off the trail. We sat down and said a little prayer, before passing the tea back and forth. As I sipped the concoction, I recall feeling how fortunate I was to be able to share this experience with Rose.

Be Here Now: Revelations and Visions

After about 20-25 minutes (The tea facilitated the onset of the trip) the effects of the mushrooms began to take hold. Surprisingly, I experienced a bit of mild anxiety at the start of this journey. The setting of my prior two psychedelic experiences had been in the predictable confines of my own apartment. After only a short way down the path, I started to feel a bit queasy. I sat down next to Rose and told her I was feeling anxious because I wasn't at "home". She looked at me with great compassion, and said that with her and Abbie by my side I was always home. I hugged both of them. After a short while, we stood up and began walking down the trail again. We traveled another quarter mile, before sitting back down on the ground. By this point, my nausea had mostly faded. However, I felt the need to close my eyes and roll with the momentum of this still emerging journey. Rose was remarkably understanding, as she seemed to sense my need to be stationary at the moment. Enchanted by the glorious sounds of nature, we closed our eyes and fell into heavy meditations. During this period, I experienced my only vision of the trip.

In this vision, I was hiking in the wilderness on the island of Maui, Hawaii. One year earlier, I had had an intense spiritual experience there. Everything in this vision felt real. I could smell the richness of the tropical salt water and hear the sweet mating calls of Hawaiian birds in the background. Most prominent of all, I saw the lush-green tree tops swaying back and forth. This vision was glorious and lasted for a few brief moments. Then, just as suddenly, I returned back to Fall Creek Falls.

After a short while, I came out of meditation and shared my vision with Rose. The following message became clear: be in the present moment. I acknowledged to her that my future fantasy is to one day live in Hawaii. I needed to learn, however, to embrace the context of my present journey. From this perspective, the future unfolds harmoniously and just as it is supposed to. Rose and I discussed this insight in some depth, and I shared with her the level of great uncertainty I was feeling about my near future. Two weeks prior, I had been unjustly dismissed from my college teaching job. After spending nearly 12 years in academia (as both a student and professor), I was feeling a bit apprehensive about life outside of it. Through Rose's wisdom, I came to see that all would be fine so long as I trusted in the ways of the Universe. Having faith meant that I had to stop thinking about the future; I had to "be here now." After what seemed like a long while, the two of us got up and continued our walk through nature. For the first time on this journey, I became keenly in tune with the majesty of our natural surroundings.

THE TREES: THEY ARE ALIVE!

The trees were brimming with so much life on magic mushrooms. Their branches seemed to reach out to me like human limbs. As I stared up at the trees, there was not a doubt in my mind that these glorious beings had souls. Why hadn't I felt this deeply before? To be sure, I had always admired nature. In this exalted state, I was fully present among the trees. I regarded them as part of my own being. We were one. I turned my head back to watch R ose, as she seemed even more entranced by our lively, green friends. She was smiling and laughing as she bounced back and forth from tree to tree. Rose would momentarily stop to hug one, then continue again. The term "tree hugger", could not be more aptly applied here!

I walked over to one of the trees and put my arms around it. I bowed my head against its massive trunk and whispered the words, "I love you" to it. I then closed my eyes and pictured our energy merging together. At that moment, I began to feel a stream of currents flow from the tree to my own head. They (the vibrations) were slow, steady, and soothing. With my eyes still closed, I began to make out the shapes and patterns of its vibrations. They appeared to me as flowing waves of red and blue circles. When I focused on sending energy to the tree, it came in the shades of blue. The tree transferred a reddish colored chi in return. I pulled my head back from the tree and opened my eyes. I stared at it in awe. Its limbs hung more expressively than ever, and its leaves were an even brighter shade of green than before. I recognized that our two souls were communicating. It seemed to be conveying this message to me:

> "It took you long enough to acknowledge my true presence. But its ok... you were distracted. I love you, too".

I turned to steal a quick look at Rose. She appeared mesmerized by our earthy friends. I then focused my attention back on the tree and fell into deep contemplation. I thought of how trees poetically capture the essence of non-duality. They are imposing but also docile. While they all eventually succumb to sickness and death, just as we all do, they continue to nourish and sustain life during their decomposition. From a spiritual standpoint, humans have much to learn from them. Too often, we get muddled in dualistic thinking. He is bad or good, or she is kind or cruel. What if one is neither good or bad, nor kind or cruel? What if, like the tree, they just are? We perpetually apply labels when all we need is to reserve judgment and accept things as they are. Adopting the way of the tree would go a long way toward cultivating true compassion.

Rose had also been thinking along the same lines. We shared our insights, and invented a silly scenario in which a group of overly rational humans interview a soulful tree. We joked about how their questions would reflect dualistic thinking. Then we discussed how the tree would have such simple yet enlightened responses. The mock interview went something like this:

Man: Tree. What are your thoughts about life? Do you have any hopes or regrets about it?

Tree: (after a long pause) Where is the sun?

Man: It's around here somewhere. See, tree, we are always debating about the true nature of humans. Are we innately bad or good? What are your thoughts?

Tree: (after long silence) I love you.

Man: Well, um, thank you. So it would appear that both the rain and the sun have its positives and negatives. Which do you prefer?

Tree: I love the sun and the rain.

Man: Well, surely you have at least a small preference?

Tree: I love the rain and the sun.

Man: Ok, I see... well then tell me what your favorite species is in the wild. Do you have a favorite one?

Tree: We are one.

Following this silly skit, Rose and I launched into a conversation about nature and awareness. We discussed how trees were content with just being in the moment and in fact know nothing of "past" or "future." We also talked of how they know little of ego. Trees do not aspire to become something other than what they are. They do not seek to become mountains in the same sense that some people cling to the illusion of becoming rich and famous. Nor does the tree contemplate such questions like how big it could have grown had it soaked up more sunlight. Instead, the tree is happy with what it is now. By this stage of the journey, the key theme became apparent: be here now. Jonathan's odyssey was an example of this theme in action. Before we continued our walk, I thought of how beautiful it was to have such an insight reinforced in Mother Nature. Prior to this journey, I had always held reverence for the wild. Now, I regarded it as SACRED.

Confronting a Stampede with Acceptance

Rose and I sat down under a tree and absorbed the moments that we had just encountered. Suddenly, a stampede of people appeared behind us. We turned around and saw a group of at least thirty fast approaching. On mushrooms, one's senses become greatly amplified. So much so that Rose and I felt their vibrations. Combined, they sounded like a stampede of elephants hurrying forth for dinner. With the group now turning the corner, I grew paranoid and told Rose that we should try and pick up the pace to remain ahead of them. We shifted gears into a fast walking speed. After a couple minutes of power walking, Rose turned to me and asked why we were trying so hard to create separation? I responded dramatically: "You can hear their vibrations too. Their energy is just way too strong right now". Rose calmly explained to me that running from them would be (metaphorically) like running from life. So, the two of us stopped walking and stood to the side of trail and waited for them to pass.

The group was a diverse lot and represented several nationalities. Prior to our journey, we saw this group huddled together praying. It was clear that they were here for the same purpose to commune with nature as we were. While their collective group energy was a bit overwhelming, it was also warm and loving. The sheer diversity of their entourage was a metaphorical reminder that it takes all kinds in the world. In response to our greetings, several among them responded in kind with waves, smiles, and quiet "hellos." I can only imagine what this group must have been thinking. Did they know that the two of us were in the throes of a mystical mushroom trip in the forest? Did we look ridiculous just standing to the side and waving? Maybe, it would have been less awkward to just go ahead of them?

After the stampede of people passed, we waited a few moments to re-collect ourselves. As we made our way back toward the trail head, we came upon a majestic waterfall down below in a canyon. We lost ourselves in the beauty of the moment. Next to the waterfall, a group of people swam. From our vantage point, these humans looked so small and inconsequential. Rose and I discussed how our culture elevates the human race above the rest of nature. Yet, in doing so, we commit an affront against creation. Far from being superior to the rest of the natural world, man is no more or less important than the wolves, the rocks, or the trees. Rose then brought our conversation back full circle to the talk we had with Jonathan one day earlier: man over complicates things.

We talked of our attachments to cars, phones, and TVs, and of how humans become further detached from their own souls. We also discussed how everything we need to connect with God is already found within us. In nature, we find a direct pathway to the Divine. After a bit of contemplation, I tried something of an open-eyed meditation and just centered my awareness upon the serenity of the moment. In so doing, I arrived at insights with regard to two perennial questions:

* How do I as an individual being fit in with creation?
* What is my life's purpose?

In the weeks and months prior to this trip, I had had a growing certainty as to these answers. However, high up on this ledge (and with the assistance of magic mushrooms) they became crystal clear. My role is the same as every being: to find their path back to Oneness. This way back is to be found through cultivating its presence within us. Only then may we come to embrace this beautiful yet difficult truth to recognize: we are all one. All of us. Even those people who we may find repulsive. The equally preposterous notions of racism and nationalism are illusions. So, too, are our separations based on material acquisition. Further, mainstream organized religion, with all its frightening divisiveness, is perhaps that grand illusion visited upon humanity. How can the worship of a great creator, who knows only love, result in horrid displays of fear, intolerance, and hate? How can the celebration of something as inspiring as the Eternal One, be converted into the egoistic ends of greed and control?

Once we discover that we are at one with each other, why stop there? If humans are interconnected, then why wouldn't the whole of humanity be so with the rest of the wild? When our species comes to this revelation, drastic changes in how we relate to nature will occur. Done will be the days of depleting our rain forests and natural habitats. Mountain top removal and global warming will become prominent issues among the public. Nuclear energy projects will be promptly shut down and an immediate apology by its proponents will be issued to the indigenous populations of the world. Demand for bottled water will plunge, as that industry's exploitive ways are revealed for all to see. Oil drilling and the corrupt power bases which control such projects will seize to exist. Gone, too, will be the poisonous influence of pharmaceutical and fast food corporations. The structure known as the state, will collapse as people come to see the illusion that is the great sorcerer unveiled.

In short, we are destined to revert back to a form of social organization akin to some of the surviving indigenous tribes of the world today. These were my thoughts while overlooking that breathtaking waterfall. Viewed from this perspective, my life's higher purpose also began to take form: to help our brethren remember that we are all one. I am to convey this point through the mediums of both writing and speaking. I was sent here to be one teacher (among many) in the spiritual revolution that is just now beginning to unfold.

After much contemplation on these existential questions, I turned to have a good look at Abbie. She was standing guard on the path to the waterfall. Throughout our journey, she acted as our noble guide. She stood watch when we first sipped the tea. She also paced herself only feet ahead of us when she normally darts out in front. Sensing our apprehension of the 'stampede', Abbie grew defensive when she thought they came to close to us. It was apparent to Rose and I that Abbie was fully aware that we were operating at a heightened sense of perception. Whether or not she knew how we got there is beside the point. More interesting, was that she seemed to be reading our energy. This led me to revisit a question about the relationship between mankind and animals. If animals are more in tune with the nuances of the spiritual plane, does that mean psychedelics will help one arrive at their same level of consciousness? Still sitting atop the waterfall, I thought long and hard on this question. Finally, I concluded that yes, they will bring you closer to their level. I arrived at this conclusion based on our own interactions with Abbie.

Following this moment of Zen, the three of us started to make our way back to the car. By this point, we had just over a mile to go on our walk. The mushrooms were starting to wear off and dusk was approaching. Our magical journey was coming to an end. We made our way down the trail, and stopped at various points to pay homage to the trees. Along the way, we also encountered a friendly couple that we stopped to talk to. We told them of Jonathan and his incredible odyssey by bicycle. We also spoke of the mushroom tea and of how we had gone on a journey. They were fascinated by our story. In turn, they told us of their own zip line adventures and favorite places to hike. We all smiled warmly at one another, shook hands, and eventually went off our own ways.

After a short while, Rose and I returned to the car and drove the two miles back to our campsite. Not long after our return, we took turns taking showers. When it was her time to bathe, I sat quietly in the tent and began to reflect on the day's journey. I crafted a poem that was to be an ode to Jonathan, the inspiring bicyclist and connoisseur of mushroom tea:

"Be Here Now"
A divine being
On his bicycle
Packing...
Mushrooms, tea, and honey
His destination?
Where ever NOW may take him
His Odyssey inspires

A great remembrance
Of who we once were
And of what we are becoming
The eternal message:
Let go of all distractions
And...
Be
Here
NOW!

THREE JOURNEYS: ONE UNIVERSAL TRUTH

Each of the three psychedelic journeys taught valuable lessons. In the DMT experience, the primary revelation was that life's essence is love. For it provides the foundation of our soul's expression. In the first mushroom trip experience, insights about the importance of letting go and embracing one's suffering emerged. In the encounter with mushroom tea, the key revelation had to do with becoming present. Taken together, each of the three themes added up to a simple but universal truth about Oneness and of how to achieve it.

We exist so that we may find ourselves back to Oneness. For our soul to remember this true reality, we have to first acknowledge that *IT's* light is already within us to begin. If it is present in our own being, then it is so in others. Arriving at this perspective has proved difficult. Why? Because we currently preach intolerance rather than acceptance. As the rot of bigotry takes hold, belief systems like racism, sexism, and nationalism emerge, spawning grave consequences for the whole of humanity. Such intolerance is rooted in fear. To which the only antidotes are radical acceptance, forgiveness, and understanding. In turn, each of these positive vibrations are grounded in the foundation of love.

Our collective inability to "just be" in the present moment also creates barriers to achieving oneness. As a result of the countless distractions in our society we are, as musician Austin Smith wrote, "Living in an Age of

Distractions." How can we countervail the force of ego with love, if we are unable to embrace what is right in front of us? Humanity must re-learn how to let go of suffering through being in the NOW.

Something must also be said for the crucial role that psychedelics can play in one's own journey. They can help unmask the ego's manifestations, and as the great spiritual teacher Ram Dass notes, help free us from the traps of our minds. Unfortunately, psychedelics are not readily available in countries like the United States, where they are strictly prohibited by authorities. For a nation who purports to uphold "freedom of religion", the use of psychedelics for spiritual practice, are strictly regulated (as in the case of Native American tribes), or outlawed all together. It is plain to see why the government would fear its use. If everyone in the country were to responsibly use psychedelics, they would quickly come to see our rulers as immoral. The Government's efforts to ban these altered states of reality, amounts to what Graham Hancock calls a "war on consciousness".

The attack on this sovereign right, by such government sponsored charades like the "War on Drugs", should be actively and openly resisted. The day is not far off when society will discard these ill-fated policies all together. Regardless of the obstacles put in their path, people will continue to gain access to and use psychedelics. Thus, spurring on many awakenings to come.

Prohibition be damned!

Poetry

A Grateful Sorrow
If the leaves could speak they would sing a harmonious tune
One of gratitude for the summer's past and the autumn's harvest
But the majestic leaves would also sing a melancholic line
Of anticipated sadness for a season's end and an impending death
But leaves would also reveal a profound and wise resonance
In their song
For in the late autumn's demise they come to appreciate nature's way
Of a mysterious yet fixed cycle:
Inception, beauty, death, and rebirth
The leaves would title their opus:
"a grateful sorrow".

The World is Your Oyster
The stillness of the majestic forest
Awakens all aspects of being
To a true and divine revelation
The world is always your oyster
Always has been and always will be
But how to act upon this knowing?
Look to the God
That is found within
And in time you will discover
The first rule of the Law of Attraction

RULE 1: Action springs from the soul's intentions

So shout aloud your intentions to the universe!
But ground them first in absolute awareness
Now go on
And seize....
The world as your oyster.

The Crossing
Do you see what I see too?
The lush green trees
Great givers of life
Do you smell what I smell too?
The heavenly aroma
Of a spring time in bloom
Do you hear what I hear too?
The peaceful sounds
Of God's chirping chorus
Do you feel as I feel too?
A sudden knowing
That we are both one
You, enchanted being
Who is down below
And me strange creature
Who is up high
Share a sacred tie...
As guardians
Of the Earth.

Becoming
What is this feeling of becoming?
A Heavenly switch flips on inside
What is wrong and what is right?
Allow the spirit to be your guide

How do I manifest my life's vision?
By embracing your power of creation
Stay aware and be ever present
To the eternal act of becoming.

The God of Love
A mystical source that cannot be known but only experienced
A transcendent power that knows nothing of fear- only love
A gentle presence that finds beauty in all things
That are natural and pure
A divine energy that does not recognize drawn boundaries
Or separateness
The humble creator that does not demand worship
Only voluntary contemplation
An open being that knows nothing of one "truth"
Only infinite shades of gray
There are multiple paths to connect to its guidance
But even more to relate
For the God of our age is the God from within....
Expressed as oneness

Becoming: A Mantra
Indeed we are
Indeed we are
Indeed we shall
Indeed we shall
Indeed we are
Indeed we are
Becoming
Becoming!

A Soulful Discovery
Radiant waves of love
Flow through our being

A connection
To the omnipresent source

That is one

And in our inquiries
Of the soul's divine
We discover truths
Into the nature of time
The Past is but a memory
And the future an escape
From the present that is already
Inside.

Progress
A gentle but transcendent knowing
Outlasting our tepid holdings
Over the sands of time...
But how to connect to this presence?
When Industry tames her power
Converting natural wonders
    Into junk.
    Behold:
The great Illusion that we call:
    "Progress".

Wandering Spirit
Wandering with no place to go
Roaming with no place to find
Freedom for thy restless spirit
From these constraints of time
    For...
What is the clock?
But a clever ploy

To divert one's soul
From the present
That is now?
So to you gentle being I say:
Let your spirit wander
Through the green majestic meadows
That lead high upon the mountain tops
And like the wild buffalo
Never stop roaming.

Reflections of Wonder
God's love is found within
But its wonders are reflected
In the calm stillness of the woods we share
The embodiment of perfection…
The trees, water, and mountains provide
Our church's true foundation
The mystic doe and song bird's cry
Stirs the soul's temptation.

Humbled
Man has iPhones, Televisions and talking wires….
Nature has awesome sunsets, majestic trees and soothing streams…
Man has automobiles and flying machines to take him places….
Nature has no place to be but here and now…
Man has clocks and watches to help him tell time….
Nature has intuitive sense that time is cosmically eternal
Man has wars for greed, conquest, and control
Nature has only unconditional love
            Man has……….
        Nothing left to strive for
            In the presence
                Of God.

A Spiritual Vision of Sustainability

IT IS IMPERATIVE FOR OUR human family to undergo a collective shift in vision of how we interact with and relate to the natural world. Only then, will we be able to address the underlying issue that has placed Mother Earth in great peril: humanity's calculated removal of its kind from the great web of creation. A prevailing, though subtle assumption among a culturally influential segment of the "developed" world, is that the planet was put here for the sole fulfillment by man. The very fact that we were endowed with the capacity to reason was proof enough that the planet was designed to be our domain. It came to follow then, that the planet was to be tamed and its nurturing elements extracted and consumed by man. The philosophical assumption that it is our right to subdue the earth is reinforced by narrow readings of scripture by religious authorities. These prevailing narratives place man at the center of creation and relegate the natural world to that of a backdrop for "HIS" activity.

This cultural narrative is also bolstered by the work of political, economic, and intellectual elites who hail the so called "virtues" of a consumer culture predicated on the exploitation of the natural world. Cultural managers deceptively package the tenants of this ideology to the greater society at large and call it "progress." Yet, a persistent question has always nagged at the various purveyors of Dominant Culture: isn't it entirely possible that man is merely part and parcel of a cosmic scheme so intricately and divinely woven that it defies our own comprehension?

Adherents of this "alternative" theory, such as the Native Indigenous Tribes of North America, contend that human beings are only one, among many, life forms. No more or less important than the tree, the bee, or the mountain. Further, man cannot be said to fully know himself until there is communion with the natural world. For it is out in the wilderness where we learn clues about our own being. From the two cultural assumptions come radically distinct visions of our relationship to the natural world; and from each arise two contrasting models of action. Both perspectives produce indirect and direct consequences for all of humanity and the natural world.

THE TWO VISIONS:

Daniel Quinn, the influential author of the eco-spiritual classic, <u>Ishmael,</u> coined the terms "Takers" and "Leavers", to refer to the two conflicting visions that arise from the assumptions (above) of mankind's relationship to nature. As their name implies, the Takers are a reference to Western Culture's encroachments upon nature. Quinn argues that the dominant western paradigm views the natural world as something to be manipulated, conquered, and exploited. In this model, man is the master and nature is the subordinate. This vision derives from a highly egotistical assumption: that man stands alone, front and center, of creation. Not surprisingly, the Taker philosophy has grave consequences for the sanctity of nature. Because it is deemed as a "right" to exploit the Earth's resources, little sensitivity is displayed by cultural architects for the issue of sustainability. For such a commitment conflicts with the culture's guiding vision of unlimited expansion and growth. As one might expect we then find entire systems put into action that not only ignore this concern but actually exasperate the problem.

The Taker vision is embodied in the consumer driven economy of today. Consumerism emphasizes unsustainable resource extraction, the re-orienting of a focus rooted in nature to that of human activity, and the mentality of conquest. The consequences of this outlook are there for all of us to see: the rapid extinction of species the world over, catastrophic nuclear leaks and oil spills, the depletion of the world's rain forests and deforestation, the poisoning and over-extraction of water, the polluting of the oceans, and the melting of the polar ice caps. This is all to say nothing of the more hidden but profound side effects of this vision. We have severed our communion with nature and suffered spiritually as a result.

In sharp contrast to the Takers, are the nature centered vision of the Leavers. For Quinn, the latter represent the original and long traveled road of human existence. The Leavers include much of the world's indigenous populations and those who live in a state of oneness with nature. Unlike the dominant Taker culture, the Leavers see the natural world as something to honor, worship, and care after. Significantly, they seek insight into the existential questions of life through nature. The Leavers view man as intricately bound to the green oasis. While they embrace the joys and wonder of the human form, it is done from a place of great reverence for the planet. The late eco-spiritual writer, Thomas Berry, described the Leaver Culture philosophy the best: "The universe is a communion of subjects, not a collection of objects."

Not surprisingly, the Leaver philosophy reflects a genuine concern for the fate of our planet. Many supporters of the Leaver mindset express outrage for the Takers' careless disregard for Mother Earth. For example, in the wake of the nuclear meltdown in Fukushima, Japan, a coalition of tribal elders and medicine people from North and South America issued an urgent statement to humanity. These "spiritual people of the earth," (as they appropriately called themselves) reminded our species of the long forgotten but natural way of living in harmony with nature. In the statement, the Elders cautioned about the inevitable destruction of the natural world if the taker vision is not discarded:

"We must address the Fukushima nuclear crisis and all actions that may violate the Creator's natural law. We have reached the crossroads of life and the end of our existence".

The Elders go on to explain that the restoration of the Leaver vision will only come about when the participants of Taker Culture turn inwards upon themselves and redefine their relationship with nature. This shift in vision amounts to a spiritual revolution:

"We are the People of the Earth and are expressing deep concern for our shared future and urge everyone to awaken spiritually. We must work in unity to help Mother Earth heal so that she can bring back balance and harmony for all her children".

In order to make sustainability a part of our everyday life in this society, we will first have to experience a radical shift in our eco-spiritual vision. A good place to start, would be to present (in no uncertain terms) the vision of the Leaver culture in a fully comprehensible way to supporters of the dominant path.

"The Universal Declaration Rights of Mother Earth," a document drafted by environmental activists at the World People's Conference on Climate Change and the Rights of Mother Earth, held in Cochabamba, Bolivia, could be a useful inception point. Drafted in the format of the US Constitution, the "preamble" to the document begins with these inspiring words:

"We, the peoples and nations of Earth: considering that we are all part of Mother Earth, are an indivisible, living community of interrelated and interdependent beings with a common destiny; We gratefully acknowledge that Mother Earth is the source of life, nourishment and learning and provides everything we need to live well".

It is only a matter of time before we celebrate the virtues of this document. Our prospects for a sustainable future depends upon it.

Beat to Your Own Drum:
Embrace the Eccentric

THE TERM "ECCENTRIC" NEEDS TO be re-defined so that it can be better understood within the context of spiritual evolution. In everyday usage, eccentricity refers to behavior that is perceived as "strange" or "unusual". So to describe someone as "eccentric," we are saying that an individual tends to act in "strange and "unusual" ways. There are two significant flaws inherent in this definition.

First, by whose perception are we viewing the eccentric from? Is it from the vantage point of the eccentric's colleagues? His/her friends and family? Or is the perception being cast by various gatekeepers of the established order, religious, political, cultural authorities and the like? Certainly, one who is a close friend of and shares a similar life philosophy as a person classified as "eccentric", is less likely to see that person this way. However, an official from the gatekeeper group, who is conditioned to view any behavior that deviates from the norm as "unusual" or "strange", is more apt to characterize an individual as such. The current definition of the term is tainted with a bias of perception.

The second problem with mainstream characterizations of the term centers on the terms "strange" and "unusual" to describe the eccentric. Aside from the bias in perception issue, both terms lack historical fluidity. By this I mean that those behaviors that at one point in time were regarded as "strange" and "unusual" may not be considered so today. For example, the appearance of anti-Korean war protesters would have been perceived as "strange or unusual" in the context of the conservative 1950's. However, the anti-establishment hippies of the late Vietnam War era were not as widely viewed this way. Why? Protest activity was common at this time. Like other challenging words such as "beautiful," the term "eccentric" constantly undergoes redefinition due to the re-shuffling of moral, cultural, and societal norms over time. What is considered "eccentric" in one historical era may not be seen as such in another one.

In light of the trouble associated with this word, I propose a new definition of the term "eccentric" that is more encompassing. My new meaning of the term follows: "**One who embraces the nuances of their being**." This new definition is free from the bias in perception. In its reconfigured form, what are perceived as "strange" and "unusual" attributes of another's behavior become his/her nuances. After all, the eccentric qualities that one perceives in another are the outward expressions of that person's inner states of being. As the eccentric's nuances are available for all to see, it can also be said that the eccentric "embraces" those subtle distinctions (nuances) of their being.

Let us now be clear on what is meant by the term "being." Dictionary definitions of the term describe it as 1) "the quality or state of having existence", or 2) The most important or basic part of a person's mind or self". An even more expansive definition of "being", as provided by my philosopher friend Sean Murphy is: "**one's total experience of all aspects of reality in any given moment**". In this definition, personal experience is thought of as the essence of existence. One's state of existing derives from their interactions with both the physical and metaphysical worlds-constituting their reality. An eccentric becomes one who openly shares their unique conceptions of it (reality) with others.

The refashioning of this term has great implications within the context of the spiritual revolution just now underway. The impact of this emerging age will revolutionize the way we relate to our planet and nature, to one another, and even extending to the way we practice politics and think about the economy. There is one big catch, however. In order to evolve as a species, each of us needs to cultivate awareness from within ourselves first. Or, as long ago observed by practitioners of both eastern and indigenous faiths, collective awareness cannot be fostered until each person turns inward upon themselves.

This is the juncture, then, where eccentricity and the cultivation of an inner awareness converge. The redefined "eccentric" now fits neatly within the context of our spiritual progression. Indeed, the characteristics of this newly defined eccentric are something to be esteemed and ultimately emulated. For to be able to "embrace the nuances of one's being," one has to be at least partially aware of who they are first. This sense of inner awareness is at the heart of our species' evolution.

The old saying that "it takes all kinds" assumes new meaning today. For it will take the sharing of each of our unique insights with one another, to raise mankind's collective vibrations. Seen in this light, we are all encouraged to openly embrace and share the nuances of what makes our personal journeys unique but also as one.

In the very near future, we will come to embrace the expanded meaning of this term. In the process, we will all become eccentrics!

Reflections

A Short Address to All Creative Souls

The pull between one's false and true sense of self is a defining feature of the human experience. This existential conflict is particularly magnified in the creative arts, where one's expression can reach a wide audience. The artists, musicians, writers, and teachers must be ever watchful for the subtle but seductive trappings of the ego. Attracting followers can quickly produce the illusion that it is "you" who people are coming to view, listen to, read, or learn from. The truth is that it is the message of awakening that people are drawn to. As such, one must relate to their chosen forms of expression as conduits of God's eternal message. However, it does require humility to arrive at this perspective. To practice it means to sacrifice your ego.

Learning to be mindful of one's narcissistic impulses is just the beginning. The creative soul should also make every effort to practice what they preach. For what could be more insincere than a self-righteous expressionist? Every thought, intention, and action should reflect the divinity of the Infinite. Each swipe of the paint brush, musical note played, word written, and lesson conveyed; should reflect the same message of universal love that one finds in their own connection to creation and through all interactions with earthly beings.

An Easter Reflection

In honor of the Easter holiday, I feel compelled to reflect upon an insightful quote attributed to the Lord Jesus Christ: "heaven is within you." To me, what Jesus implies is, that there is no need to look for "saving" from a divine entity. In fact, there is no need to be "saved" at all. If we turn inwards, we will find that God is already within us. We need only to awaken ourselves to a universal truth that we are all programmed by our culture to forget: that each of us are already one with God. We can self-actualize this truth through our own inner liberation. In my humble opinion, Jesus would have disapproved of the church for transforming him into a messiah. For surely, he regarded one's path as an inward journey to salvation.

So, it also follows, that we are not the sinful beings depicted by scripture. For through eternity, heaven is within each of us all. Viewed in this light, Jesus did not die to "save" us from our "sins". He did so to show that the un-God like realities that we create on this planet (hell) through our false identifications with the ego self cannot transcend the divine qualities of spirit (heaven) that prevail within us. Jesus's choice to go through with the crucifixion was a transcendent (and heroic) lesson in action. In honor of his profound insight, I devote this night's meditation to finding the heaven that lies within.

CROSS-EXAMINING PROGRESS

We think we move forward but we take two steps back when we stray further into the technological abyss. How many of us take the time to authentically interact? To introduce ourselves to a neighbor, lend a helping hand to a stranger? Facebook, iPhones, and televisions are each distractions that prevents us from living in the moment. Technology is a well of potential at our fingertips; but it becomes our great oppressor when we fail to ground it with a spiritual foundation. Presently, it is in the service of all those values that we as a human family should deplore: fear, ignorance, greed, and separation. We secretly yearn for what is natural, but we deny ourselves these primal urges all in the empty pursuit of "progress". Let us end this unhealthy obsession with life's distractions. Strap on your boots and re-connect with Mother Nature. Return to that time when life was simple. Sing, dance, laugh, and play! Oh how wonderful that day will be when we let our spirits free!

A New Role Model

As a society, we place great emphasis on cultivating role models for our youth. Unfortunately for all of us, ours reflect the egoistic values of the culture. These principles include: celebrity fame, material wealth, physical beauty, and personal charisma. It should not be surprising to find that actors and actresses, athletes, business leaders, pop musicians, and even politicians become the objects of our youths' affection. As more of us come to awaken, we will see that our youth need new role models to emulate and loving guides to follow. The question is, who will stand in to replace our pop-culture icons?

How about parents? If they were to live more freely and were not as inhibited by societal conditioning, then possibly. Until then, most young people will go on regarding their parents as out of touch with the realities of being a child. What about teachers? Surely they play an instrumental role in the evolution of our youth. Unfortunately, many children come to regard their teachers with great suspicion. For either subconsciously or consciously, many young people believe educators are conspiring to sequester their souls. They are right! The formal education system is little more than a rigid indoctrination machine. It trains our youth to become good worker bees and consumers. Spiritual growth is relegated to the back burner. Might our church leaders come to fill this gap? How many young people WILLINGLY attend religious services?

Let's think grander. Need our new role model(s) even be in human form? After all, a case could be made that mankind is not worthy of emulation. To be sure, we are all divine children born of a most humble creator. However, as evidenced by our species' collective state of hubris, humanity is still very much in the infancy of spiritual evolution. This brings us to a more suitable candidate who also happens to be the epitome of perfection: Mother Nature. Why couldn't the majesty that is the green oasis, stand in for our standard bearers of ego? There is already a precedence for this. Scattered throughout the world, are various indigenous tribes who regard the earth as sacred. From holding her up as an idol, our youth would learn how to coexist with all beings in a peaceful and harmonious manner.

Through observing the interactions between a flower and a bee, children would learn about cooperation. From the tree it would learn about faith, for the tree trusts that rain will fall and the sun will shine. Atop the summit of a mountain, our youth would be schooled in the way of unity, as they gain a bird's eye view of how her wondrous singularities (such as the water, rocks, and trees) give form to the whole of a picture perfect mosaic. Finally, the child would learn of truth. They will see that no being in the natural world lives by way of deception. Each act as they are intended to by God. The snake hunts and kills frogs and rodents to survive. It is not ashamed of who he is by nature. Nor does the tree dress up as a mountain so that she may impress the river. The tree is content with just being it.

Most importantly, elevating nature to that of a societal icon would make us all more loving and compassionate beings. Let us set out together to spread the word that we have re- anointed an old and long lost role model: The Earth.

The Mystical Experience of Love

LOVE IS A DIVINE POWER. It is also an awareness that God's presence is found in everything and in everyone. As the essence of our being, its energy resonates at the highest levels in the Universe. Love also transcends all dualities, as it is a reflection of both the rain and the sun. Love also knows nothing of the temporal boundaries of space or time. Its vibrations are eternal. Since it springs from the divine, love also underlies all modes of our thoughts, interactions, and acts of creation. It comes to signify our communion with spirit. Love finds its expression through profound displays of passion, and in personal revelations and acts of genuine compassion. Love is even manifested in moments of deep suffering. If embraced, the flame of inspiration is lit.

Just as love has different vehicles of expression, so too, does it take many forms. The four types of love most **familiar** (The Ancient Greeks conceived of numerous categories of love) to us can be called familial, friendship, romantic, and mystical love. The first three should be more generally known and are easily recognized. The fourth is the least understood and identified, but extends full meaning to each of the former. Unfortunately, many obstacles (of our own creation) frustrate blissful moments of it. Thankfully, several age old techniques and practices help us re-connect to its presence. Below is a description of these four forms of love, with an emphasis on the transcendent aspects of the mystical kind.

The Four Forms of Love

Familial Love

Familial love is the tender touch one extends to a kin. We might think of the relationship between a parent and their child or of siblings. It even extends to the special bond between a pet owner and their animal. Familial love expresses itself in a myriad of ways: with joy, empathy, and unconditional acceptance being among the most common and profound. Of the first three forms, familial love is also the most difficult to sever. The old saying that "friends come and go", does not apply to one's immediate family or tribe. The relationship between kin remains intact (though not without some difficulty) through both thick and thin. This unwavering display of loyalty, explains why the death of a child, parent, or sibling is among the most difficult losses that one can endure.

To enjoy the fruits of familial love, one must learn to sacrifice their ego. Spiritual writer, Eckart Tolle, has noted the prevalence of egoistic relationships between kin. He attributes this problem to the hyper-commercial/instant gratification culture of the West. Inner peace can be hard to come by in this society, for one's fulfillment is derived through submitting to the drives of ego: bank accounts, houses, occupational status, and the like. It is not surprising that parents frequently project their own insecurities onto children.

Sometimes, the child will even become an extension of a parent's unfulfilled yearnings and expectations. Think here of the over bearing father who emphasizes winning above all else in his son or daughter's athletic pursuits. Rather than embrace the child's participation in athletics for the sake of building comradery and teamwork, the satisfaction of his egoistic urges becomes the motivating aim. Tolle even goes as far to say, that some adults make the decision to have children to ensure the continuance of their own blood lines. Certainly, such considerations do not reflect the meaning of familial love.

As will follow below, the experience of mystical love extends greater meaning to one's familial relationships. For the love between kin is a most sacred connection. When this form cosmically flows, it is a beauty to behold. Examples of it abound: the sacrifice of a parent working overtime to ensure that their children do not go without, the family who stands behind their suffering drug addicted child/sibling, and the pet owner who arrives home for lunch to steal a cherished moment with their special companion.

FRIENDSHIP LOVE

Friendship love is the gift of repeated acts of compassion shared between two people. A good example of its beauty can be found in the bond between close friends. This attraction emerges out of one's participation in another person's moments of joy and suffering. When friendship fully matures, it becomes a perpetual exercise in loyalty and radical acceptance. Friendship love is not only restricted to long time comrades. It can also appear suddenly between onetime strangers or mere acquaintances.

An anecdotal example of friendship love occurred toward the end of my first tenure as a college professor. At that time, I struck up a close friendship with an older faculty member named Jethro. Jethro was a profoundly wise being who had lived much of his life amongst tribal peoples. Our relationship began with frequent conversations in the hallways, and gradually progressed into a close friendship. This process was cemented by one event that occurred in the spring semester of my second year at the school. One day, I was informed by the college administration that I was being dismissed from my teaching job at the semester's conclusion. I was devastated. After my last class of the day, I locked myself in my office and wept. I didn't want anyone to see me in such a vulnerable state. When I finally grew the courage to walk out, I passed somberly by Jethro's office. He saw me, and gently suggested that I sit down and talk. I then began to recount what I had just learned. When I finished speaking, Jethro looked me square in the eyes and said with great compassion: "one door closes and another one opens. You will be just fine."

Jethro's reassuring words left an imprint on my soul. He said what I needed to hear at that exact moment. For the remainder of the semester, the two of us met for lunch nearly every day and I learned the details of his own journey. He recounted such heavy events in his life, like the tragic death of his beloved wife to a car accident. We also shared several light hearted moments together. He confessed that he felt just as out of place as I did around the other faculty.

A remarkable aspect of friendship love is the spontaneous fashion in which it emerges. As a demonstration of this fact: Identify the best friend(s) in your own life and try and recall how you met. Chances are, the circumstances of your first encounter(s) with that person(s) was quite unexpected. Now, try to describe the feeling you had when meeting them. For most people, the experience might be described as something like this: "totally out of the blue, but picture perfect." Still, others might take their recollection a step further, and describe it as "destiny.... like we were supposed to cross paths."

As with familial love, the ego can appear and disrupt authentic displays of friendship. Two associated problems arise here. First, some friends settle into set roles or adopt a persona when they are around certain people. For instance, in my formally close knit group of high school friends, I played up my role as the goofy but lovable eccentric. I did so in order to be accepted by the others. In caving into my own fears of rejection, I was led astray by ego. The result? I was taken advantage of by my other "friends". They saw my exaggerated kindness as a weakness to exploit. This ties into the second problem that can plague friendship love: the need by some people to assert control over others. This desire to do so also emanates from the insecurities of the ego. In such cases, the friendship seems to revolve around only one of the parties. The principle of reciprocity is nonexistent. The value of the other friend(s) becomes measured to the extent, that they can make the dominant individual feel better about themselves.

In this type of "friendship," the ascendant person may even insult or put down the other. Such a situation is unfortunate as both parties are unable to detach from their egoistic roles as abuser and victim. Fortunately, the ego's grip on the expression of friendship love can be averted. As is possible with familial love, ego can be harnessed by the transcendent experience of mystical love. When practiced with true compassion, friendship is one of the most inspiring forms of love known to man.

ROMANTIC LOVE

Romantic love is the intimate connection shared between two kindred spirits. It blossoms through the soulful recognition of one another from past incarnations. The intense passion that romantic love evokes, has been storied through the ages. Musicians, writers, and artists of all varieties, have long tried to capture its essence in the creative form. The playwright, William Shakespeare, and the artist, Vincent Van Gogh, were just two creative souls (among many) who tried to express its dual nature of bliss and anguish.

The spiritual communion of two divine souls is expressed physically through the act of making love; and is a catalyst of this great passion. This act is made all the more poignant, because it serves as life's inception point. The beauty of this expression also infuses a transcendent quality into romance. Kindred spirits experience elements of all three forms of love. They are best friends even as they are lovers. The intensity of this connection even spawns the loyalty of the familial form. The result is a sacred trinity of unconditional love.

Similar to an initial meeting with a best friend, one with a romantic partner also leaves an indelible mark. Often, these "first" meetings appear to be remarkable for their wild spontaneity. They leave both participants with a 'knowing', of a most blissful reunion. This sense or feeling, is particularly strong in the meeting of two eternal souls or soul mates. The meeting of my own soul mate, Rose, was one such moment of dramatics. We met during a twice-weekly meditation hour on campus. From the first moment I saw her I was captivated. However, I didn't act on this feeling for a month due to a lack of courage. On the day that I delivered a lecture on campus titled the "Hippie Revival", she approached me with a magazine her mother had had from the 1970's. We laughed about its cover. It was a picture of two lovers forming a human peace sign. This was a special moment. I asked for her number and we planned our first "date" three days later. You would be correct, if you guessed that we went on a hike in the woods!

Our first "date" was what I would call "perfectly harmonious." It felt like we had known each other over the scope of several lifetimes. Rose seemed to already know everything about me that had meaning. She may have been fuzzy on the details of my present life (members of my family, when my birthday was etc.) but she understood the essence of who I was... the soul being temporarily housed in this physical vessel. On that first hike, the passion that Rose and I felt for each other was indescribable. The comfort I felt with her in moments of silence, was the tell-tale sign that she was my soul mate. Our first "date" felt much more like a reunion than an interaction of scattered and awkward moments.

Sadly, as the ego can distort the vibrations of the first two forms, so can it too with romantic love. Negative outcomes generally result when one or both partners introduce their insecurities into the relationship. In this case, two egocentric versions of romantic love emerge: In the first scenario, one or both partners subconsciously use the other as an emotional crutch. Rather than turn inward and embrace their own suffering (which can be quite painful), they look to a partner to make them happy. The obvious problem here is that one or both partners become co-dependent on the other. One cannot find inner peace through the conduit of another. They must find it within themselves first. Furthermore, soul mates were intended to be about the communion of two **separate** souls coming together as one. It is not about the surrender of one person's identity to the other. To do so would be to deny one of God's most precious gifts to us - the exercise of freewill.

The second egoistic scenario occurs when one or both partners use the relationship for the purpose of self-gain. For a society that vibrates on a very low spiritual plane, this type of relationship usually revolves around pure physical gratifications such as monetary security and personal status. The loss of a sense of self-worth is usually the end result of this type of arrangement. For one comes to see themselves more as an object of their "partners" manipulative ploy then as a source of love and affection.

As one who has found himself in both past scenarios (as both the culprit and the victim), one thing was for certain...to encounter them was awful at the time. Like all painful experiences they made for teachable life moments. From them, I came away with one truth about love and compatibility: when two peaceful souls meet, there is harmony. If two tumultuous souls combine... love is like a roller coaster on its best days! Fortunately, for all romantics everywhere, this form of love was intended to express a most sacred bond.

MYSTICAL LOVE

Mystical love is the overwhelming feeling of gratitude that one expresses for a profound and sacred moment. Of the four forms, this one is also the most intense, because it tends to inject a transcendent quality into the first three. One's encounter of mystical love, typically follows an awe-inspiring event that goes by different names. The psychologist, Abraham Maslow, famously termed it a "Peak Experience." The spiritual writer, William James, called it a "mystical state". Researchers at the Institute of Noetic Sciences, give it the name of a "Noetic Experience." Personally, I like Jame's use of the term "mystical". However, due to its typically fleeting nature, I think of it more as an experience. A combination of the two words work well. Together, they capture the "peak" feeling that Maslow tried to convey.

The mystical experience can only be described as transcendent, for one arrives at a knowing that they are amidst a higher and divine presence. Following this event, one experiences a range of emotions that includes gratitude, humility, and wonder. These feelings amount to an encounter with mystical love, as they provide glimpses into the world of spirit. In his book, <u>The Varieties of Religious Experience</u>, James notes that there are 4 key qualities of the Mystical State (experience). First, it must be directly encountered; second, it tends to reveal both personal and universal truths about divinity; third, these experiences are transitory or "fleeting"; and finally, they tend to happen spontaneously. I would personally add three qualities to James's list:

- Mystical experiences tend to take place in environments where one feels most connected
- Mystical Experiences have a dramatic effect on raising one's conscious awareness
- Mystical experiences inspire one's faith in Oneness

From meditation exercises and prayer, to psychedelic encounters, the catalysts for mystical experiences can vary. In their book, Living Deeply: The Art and Science of Transformation in Everyday Life, researchers at the Institute of Noetic Sciences discovered that baring witness to deeply existential events, like childbirth, may trigger them as well. The same researchers also found that some astronauts report having had mystical experiences while on mission in outer space. Mother Nature is also among the best known catalysts of these events.

An Example of a Mystical Experience: The Bowing Deer

Describing one's mystical experience is not always easy to put into words. This is due to its profoundly personal nature. Nonetheless, I will give it my best effort. A beautiful hike through the woods, with Rose and Abbie, was the setting of a most memorable mystical experience of mine. The three of us were walking down a trail, when about 200 feet away, a doe stopped abruptly in the middle of it. I placed Abbie on leash so that she wouldn't give it chase. Over the course of the next 30 seconds, our pack and the doe locked eyes. Suddenly, it appeared like she was trying to bow her head to us, as if acknowledging our presence. In all my time spent in nature, I had never seen any animal being do this before.

For a brief moment, I took my eyes off the gorgeous deer to see Rose bowing to it. I directed my attention back to the enchanted creature and followed suit. To our great astonishment, the doe bowed her head down to us. After a few seconds, we lowered our heads a second time to her. The same response followed. Amazed, we bowed a third time to her. Once again, the same reaction! Overcome with awe, Rose and I clasped our hands together and knelt to the ground. We honored her presence for the fourth time. Remarkably, the doe bent down as low as she could go (almost like a curtsey) and bowed back to us. By this point, we were both absorbed in the divinity of the moment. Not once, not twice, not three, but four times, the doe honored our souls! Just as astounding, was the fact that Abbie didn't tug on the leash in pursuit of it. She sat quietly, and looked on in the same wonder.

After the fourth exchange of bows, Rose and I looked at each other in disbelief as the doe turned to walk away. As a show of respect, we began to head back in the direction we came from. After taking only a few steps, the three of us looked back to see that the deer was standing again in the middle of the trail. She wished to bid us one final farewell. We waved at her. Then the doe disappeared back into the woods. Incredibly, our encounter with "bowing deer", occurred on the same day that I began writing this section on mystical love. Does this sound like a coincidence?

Each of the qualities of the mystical experience were present in our encounter. First, our interactions with the deer were directly experienced. (James' first quality). Second, We both garnered truths about the nature of divinity (James's second quality). I personally drew two existential meanings from this event.

On a cosmic level, this awesome interaction with the doe seemed to embody the unseen threads that ties us all together. Mankind and nature are not separate, but are divinely woven. The experience also served as a reminder that God regularly communicates with us through IT'S many conduits. In our mystical encounter, nature fulfilled this role. If the doe was our divine messenger, what was she trying to convey to us? In the days that followed, I tried to piece together the symbolism. On a personal level, the deer seemed to be acknowledging (approvingly) the journey I was on. As a creature who embodies gentleness, I also sensed that she symbolized the very essence of Rose. Perhaps, then, the doe was a peaceful reflection of our communion together. Also consistent with James' third quality, was the fleeting nature of this encounter. The whole interaction took place in a brief time span, perhaps five to seven minutes. In fact, had we begun the hike thirty minutes earlier, the three of us would have missed out on this encounter. As It happened, Rose ran 30 minutes late that day to meet me at the park!

This event was also spontaneous. Yet, I had a feeling that it was fated to happen. It may well be that what we call "spontaneity" is not really so at all. Maybe, it is a name we apply to describe that which we don't quite understand. A better way to refer to James' fourth quality is to say that spontaneity is an expression of cosmic flow. The setting of this encounter with "bowing deer" was also in an environment that I felt deeply connected to (the woods). In fact, a majority of all my mystical experiences have been set in the glory of nature. This interaction also broadened my overall perspective of reality. I became more confidant in my knowing that all sentient beings are one. Finally, how could one's faith in a divine wisdom not grow through such an experience?

A Window into the Experience of Mystical Love
In the days following our encounter with "bowing deer," I enjoyed immense feelings of gratitude, humility, and wonder. I felt the warm embrace of mystical love. This event had a remarkable effect on my outlook towards all earthly beings, leading me to revisit questions I had long held about animal consciousness. I wondered if "bowing deer" felt the same impact from the event as I did. Deep in my prayers and meditations, I also found myself giving thanks to God, for the godsends of my friends and family. Gratitude was not the only emotion I experienced. I began to enjoy my relationships with a renewed sense of wonder. The subtle dynamics of our interactions fascinated me. I began to pay closer attention to how I interacted with others in silence. As days went by, I continued to feel intense

waves of joy. The source of this bliss was humility. The mystical encounter with the doe so humbled me, that I distanced myself ever greater from the Atheistic mindset. The doe was a clear manifestation of Oneness.

There exists, however, one potential downside to the mystical experience. The insights that one comes away with can quickly fade if they are not grounded in daily contemplative practices like meditation/prayer, yoga, or interactions with nature. Otherwise, the first three forms of love are enriched by the humility with which these events inspire. If mystical love has the power to heal our friendships, romantic partnerships, and familial bonds, what is preventing more people from having mystical experiences? I can think of two possible responses to this question:

First, most people **do** in fact have mystical experiences. However, due to societal conditioning, many don't acknowledge that they have. Sometimes, when people report having had one, they are dismissed as "crazy" by their friends, peers, and family. Sadly, some people deny having had them at all. The fear of confronting a new reality may also deter us from having these types of experiences. Instead, we cling to what is safe and familiar in the top soil variants of physical existence. In so doing, we pass right over the more meaningful world of spirit and discount IT's divine signs.

There is also the possibility that many have not, as of yet, developed the capacity to have a mystical experience. This does not imply that they never will. All of us have this innate ability to awaken to the mystical. It is just a matter of when (not if) one's soul becomes conscience of its true and boundless self. In my own case, for example, I can only recall having had one mystical experience in the years prior to my soul's awakening (up until age thirty). Thinking back on it, I am not even sure if I regarded it as such. By comparison, I have had countless such experiences in the short space of time since.

This does beg the question: was I just simply unaware of having had mystical experiences when I was younger; or did I only start to have them once I began to awaken? The good news is that this question does not need answering. This is due to the presence of age-old wisdom practices that increase one's odds at having a mystical experience. Below are brief descriptions of three that have worked for me. This list is not all encompassing.

MEDITATION

Meditation is the process by which one unlocks the key to their inner self. This feat is accomplished through the act of focused contemplation. As an ancient practice, meditation is intended to serve two intertwined functions. The first, is the silencing of one's ego through stillness of mind. When we "sit" we abandon the ego's obsessive thoughts over the past and quell its fear-based projections of the future. In place of both, one centers their attention on the here and now. In so doing, we embrace the one reality that our soul knows: eternity. Time is always unfolding, and we are constantly becoming. Notions of "past "and "future", are mere inventions of the ego. As expressed so eloquently by Kahlil Gibran, author of The Prophet:

"Yesterday is but today's memory and tomorrow is today's dream".

In becoming more present in the moment, we also grow more aware of the intentions underlying our thoughts, actions, and behaviors. If we practice consistently enough, we also come to gradually detach ourselves from mindless distractions. With a clear awareness, we can't miss out on having a mystical experience! Meditation can, in and of itself, also induce a mystical event. Throughout the ages, people have experienced phenomenon during this unique form of prayer which can only be described as awesome. These reports include everything from out of body experiences and astral travel to premonitions. Through meditation, some spiritual masters have even gleaned knowledge of their past incarnations. For anyone who has sat in for a group meditation will know, the vibrations of love are fully palpable. This expressed energy flows from a most Supreme Source. IT's access points are found within.

Nature

"I Submit"
No man can command my respect
For that is something that must be earned
But nature can command my respect
With her soft whispers and thunderous crashes
And she enchants me with her wet caresses
She feasts upon the ego's lifeblood
And as unconsciousness turns to consciousness
I become aware
That nature is always there.

The qualities of nature inspire the soul's awakening. Through her many wonders, we come to learn clues about our own being. Time spent in nature provides us with a remedy against the ills that currently plague humanity. For it is the essence of love and the spirit of eternity. The natural world provides fertile ground for mystical experiences. All one has to do is acknowledge her signs to attract them. One may connect to the Earth in countless ways. Hiking, swimming, mountain biking, and climbing are just a few. Activities like bird watching or photography can also provide the same fertile ground for connection. Try setting aside 45 minutes to 1 hour every day to interact with the natural world. In short time, you may very well have your own mystical experience to share.

CREATIVE EXPRESSION

Through the sacred act of creating, we access our inner God. One's mode of creative expression need not matter. Art, music, writing, photography, theatre, dance, gardening etc.; all serve as avenues that nurture our souls. When we find ourselves lost in the depths of our own expression (the artist who suddenly becomes obsessed with a painting), our souls are inspired. In a 2006 letter to a high school class, the late Kurt Vonnegut (celebrated author-essayist), urged the students to create for the sake of self-spiritual exploration:

> *"Practice any art, music, singing, dancing, acting, drawing, painting, sculpting, poetry, fiction, essays, not to get money and fame, but to experience <u>becoming</u>, to find out what is inside of you, <u>to make your soul grow</u>".*

Through heeding the wise words of Vonnegut, we may all increase our odds of having mystical experiences. Why? Because creative expression has the effect of expanding one's wonder for the world. Through the act of "becoming," that creativity engenders, one's soul easily opens up to new experiences as they occur. Finally, if one is tuned in to the existential meanings behind their creative acts, they will find that it is impossible to **not** have mystical experiences. For creativity itself, stems from the very depths of the sacred and mystical.

MYSTICAL LOVE AND THE HEALING OF HUMANITY

We can heal humanity through experiencing mystical love. The feelings of awe that it inspires can repair our broken relationships. Mystical events leave us with a knowing that we are all part of something much greater. When we discover this truth, our identification with the ego gradually withers away. The negative qualities of fear dissolve into the positive vibrations of hope. Aside from producing happier people, mystical love also has the power to forge global unity, that unspoken recognition that we are all children of the same God. Mystical love can heal the way we relate to and approach our familial relationships, friendships, and romantic partnerships. The moral rot that pervades much of the world, stems from a lack of love in those three areas. The first three forms of love exist solidly on their own; but they each become embodiments of the ONE when infused with the inspiring mystical quality. When we come to internalize this truth we will achieve:

HEAVEN on EARTH.

Haiku

The happy dog glistens
In the stream below
An inspiring girl.

The running stream
Swift like a leopard's stride
The beauty of creation.

Naked Rose wades in water
Curious dog follows
A Glorious day.

Dog chases stick
Faster than the speed of sound
A divine flash of white.

The Doe bows its head with grace
Her three kin look on in wonder
Oneness.

Delightful meadows
Sing melodies to my soul
Church is in nature.

Inspired beings
Meet high upon the summit
NAMASTE to you!

A Crisp mountain air
Whistles through to my essence
The bliss of being.

Clear blue colored skies
Convey an absolute truth
The light shines inside.

Stillness is present
In green majestic fields
Home of bowing deer.

The hidden trail
Beckons the soul to follow
Paradise awaits.

Wind's gentle whispers
Breaths peace and tranquility
A season's greeting.

Earthy spirit sings
To the serenity of the day
Blessed she is.

Winter's breath is cold
But it pulls our attention
To this moment.

Bright sky consumed by grey
Storm clouds take their turn
To Earth's godly rhythms.

Water fills the creek with love
Gentle calm is born anew
Silent still.

Sun casts its shadow
Upon hollowed trees below
Mystic moon rises.

Spirited wings of God
Glides heavenly through the sky
Ode to eagle!

Butterfly spreads its wings
To my great delight
An ancestor's greeting.

Fool's machine of hubris
Flies arrogantly through sky
Faults of progress.

Hippie Spirituality

———

THE GENERAL PUBLIC ARE FAMILIAR with surface level characteristics of hippie culture. Their dress attire, music taste, and mannerisms are identifiable to most people. Little is understood, however, about the nuances of their spiritual beliefs, practices, and aspirations. After all, the defining characteristic of any cultural sub group lies in the manner in which they worship God. For there is nothing greater or of more importance, than one's connection to their Creator. This also holds true in the world of "hippiedom". Spirituality, is the most significant aspect of what it means to be a "hippie." What follows is a brief description of what I term "Hippie Spirituality".

In writing on this topic, I do not claim to speak for the spiritual beliefs, practices, and aspirations of **all** people who identify as hippies. Instead, it is my intent to paint a more general overview of the key tenets informing hippie spirituality. My personal goal is to help correct any misconceptions that people may have about it. Dominant culture has so thoroughly discredited what it means to be a hippie, that many (but by no means all) associate them with the mainstream's disparaging depictions. Being a hippie is about much more than growing long hair, rejecting social norms, and smoking copious amounts of ganja. It is about one's faith in and connection to the Divine. The following is a list and description of ten tenets (10 tenets easy to remember!) in hippie spirituality.

Tenet 1: The Earth is Sacred

At the root of hippie spirituality is a belief that the Earth is sacred. The forests, mountains, oceans, and rivers are regarded as holy spaces of communion with God. All of Mother Earth's creatures are revered and venerated as humble teachers of life. The hippies' deep and heartfelt love of the wild extends out into the wider culture at large, and is felt through some of the following causes and endeavors: an emphasis on sustainability, opposition to fossil fuels and nuclear power, concerns about over population, and the promotion of wild life preservation. Hippies are advocates for all God's creatures and embrace their roles as activists of the Earth.

The love of nature so moves hippies that they often feel compelled to move away from the urban centers (where the Hippie counterculture actually originated) and into the countryside or mountains. Some of the most genuine hippies one will find reside in those natural places where one's connection with God is unfettered by the kinds of distractions found in cities. Not surprisingly, many hippies spend a good portion of their time outdoors engaged in soul-enriching activities like hiking, biking, mountain climbing, and swimming.

As hippies connect to God through the Earth, they also come to admire and incorporate the spiritual framework of their true ancestors (and forerunners) into their own outlooks on divinity. Of course, the ancestors I speak of are the Native Americans. These infinitely wise souls not only regard the Earth as sacred, but have long taught that the separate notions (in our minds) of God, Earth, and Mankind are actually one. The Native Americans regard the Earth as the purest manifestation of God's creation. Conversely, they also see the spirit of God embedded in the holy landscapes of the wild. It goes without saying that Earth Day for hippies is akin to Christmas or Easter for Christians. It is an occasion to honor that which gives and nourishes life.

Tenet 2: God is an Open Being who defies our Depictions of *IT*

Most hippies believe that God is a loving being who accepts multiple paths to its omnipresent source of light. In other words, one does not have to follow a prescribed for set of rituals or attend a church to commune with IT's divine energy. This innate freedom to worship as one chooses has seen the hippies delve into the practice of spiritual faiths as diverse as Buddhism and Hinduism (both of which originated in the East), Rastafari (which began in Jamaica in 1930), Native American mysticism (which draws on the earth-centered practice of shamanism), New Age spirituality (which draws its philosophy from an assortment of faiths), and even Christian and Sufi mysticism. For example, a group of hippies from the 1960's, known as the "Jesus people", emerged to live directly the teachings of Jesus Christ. This mystic sect also moved off the land to escape the authoritarian influence of the Church. Sound familiar?

Hippies have also maintained that God cannot be pigeon-held by man's narrow and egoistic conceptions of IT. Most hippies would not assign our own physical attributes to describe the Eternal One. In other words, God is not just an old man with a beard who lives high in the sky. Nor does God cast judgment upon or carry out vengeance against those who displease IT. A hippie would say that God is unconditional love. While the universal law of Karma (what you put out you receive back) applies, it is we who punish ourselves with our own negative deeds. There is no deity that sits above tallying our good and evil acts. God is also not a "HE". The Great Spirit knows nothing of gender. IT is better described as a presence that can take countless forms like: a mountain or sunset, the moment of child birth, or an inspiring musical performance and piece of art work.

TENET 3: SKEPTICISM OF DOMINANT CULTURE'S RELIGION

Hippies have long had a conflicted relationship with the West's dominant religion, Christianity. On the one hand, many hippies regard the Prophet, Jesus Christ (The object of Christian worship), with great love and admiration. With good reason. For in the truest sense, Jesus was a hippie long before the coining of the term. This divine messenger was a tireless wanderer of spirit. By some accounts, Jesus traveled to distant lands as far east as India to learn from Buddhist mystics and spread the word of God. Jesus was also a humble teacher who preached against vanity and self-righteousness. As a passionate defender of the world's poor and downtrodden, Jesus taught to live simply. Above all, he saw that God was present in all aspects of creation and sought to communicate how we are all one.

Hippies take no issue with those who honor Jesus. Rather, they are cynical of the institutional structure that formed (long ago) around the image of Christ. Many hippies contend, that high authorities (Priests, Kings, and Bishops) co-opted Jesus' original teachings in order to gain political power and influence. As the church's past and bloody record of inquisitions against "non-believers" show, they achieved their objectives with startling success. From the onset, power hungry church leaders and politicians learned how to morph this inspiring man into a cult-like figure of control. By most historical accounts, Jesus actually held a deep suspicion of organized structures of authority and spoke out against the folly of worshiping other men. For he believed that the spirit of the Divine was found within.

Hippies have also critiqued the Church's own conceptions of God for assigning personal attributes to IT, which reflect the ego's thirst for power. Christianity's version of God, is a wrathful deity who assigns judgment, exacts revenge, demands conformity to "HIS" will, and extols the natural order of hierarchy. In reality, God does none of those things. For IT is the embodiment of unconditional love, forgiveness, freedom, and oneness. Unfortunately, when hippies point out the contradictions between the intuitive God of love and the external God of fear, they are commonly portrayed by Church propagandists as threats to the moral structure of society. This irony is lost on no one. I have personally met and befriended several Christian raised hippies (I was also one them) who point out the Church's contradictions. Many of these same people also devote their lives trying to emulate the personal qualities and character of Jesus. In so doing, they are embodiments of his beautiful spirit.

Tenet 4: World Peace is Attained Through the Discovery of Inner Peace

Peace, love, and unity is much more than a catchy slogan that hippies repeat out of habit. Rather, this phrase captures a key facet of hippie spirituality. To be sure, there is much discussion and disagreement among hippies about how world peace is achieved. Some believe that this heavenly state is attained by resisting society's warmongers (See Government) through non-violent- direct protest. While protesting draws attention to the evils that perpetuate global disharmony, it alone cannot bring about world peace.

Other hippies believe that the absence of peace is a spiritual issue rather than a political one. This line of thought holds, that the world will only achieve the utopia of "peace, unity, and love", when man acknowledges that peace within themselves first. This revelation has inspired many hippies to identify the nature of their own suffering. In the hopes of fulfilling such a quest, they have since the 1960's, incorporated Eastern teachings into their broad, spiritual framework. Despite their nuances, Hinduism and Buddhism both share an emphasis on the eternal nature of suffering and of how to transcend it by looking within. The world would be a more peaceful place, if we could each discover our inner house of refuge.

Tenet 5: Meditation as a Key to Unlock Your Inner God

Hippies have widely embraced the practice of mediation since the 1960's, when Eastern Yogis descended upon the United States in droves. Meditation is a form of prayer that attempts to quiet the mind from the ceaseless thoughts and distractions that prevents us from being present. Being in the NOW, affords us all two things: first, it allows us to be in tune with our suffering. When the mind is no longer trapped in yesterday's moments of regrets, or consumed by worries of future events that have not yet transpired, we can access the range of emotions that we are really feeling. We take the first steps to finding inner peace when we access those depths of being where suffering lies.

There is also a second and (arguably) deeper purpose behind the practice, which often goes overlooked by meditation teachers in the west. Meditation serves as a direct inner pathway to God. I have personally experienced and met people who have had extraordinary occurrences during meditation. Some of which include: spiritual visions, the ability to send healing to others, out of body experiences, and feelings of vibrational oneness with the Universe. Each of these occurrences can only be described as forms of divine communion. One cannot, however, hope to fully connect with God during the course of their meditation, until they learn to be present. It is only in NOW when we encounter Oneness.

Tenet 6: Emphasis on Spirit of Service to all Beings

Hippies place great emphasis on the spirit of service to all beings. Some of these compassionate acts include: coming to the aid of a neighbor in need, extending sympathy to a person who is suffering, and extending one's forgiveness to another. Hippies believe that each act of good will amounts to a positive change in the world, no matter how small or inconsequential one's act may appear to be. The positive impact on the planet is profound when two or more people direct their energy toward a noble cause. One example of such an impact was the Farm's earthquake relief mission in Guatemala. There, several members from the hippie commune in Summertown, Tennessee, helped rebuild damaged homes caused by the natural disaster. The volunteers' impact on the impoverished country side was both instantaneous and (by the Farm's own accounts) widely appreciated by the village inhabitants.

The anti-Vietnam protest movement of the 1960's-70's is another example from the same time period which saw hippies band together to inject much needed positivity into the world. During these protests, countless young hippies rose up to demand an end to that hellish and immoral conflict. Eventually, they persevered. After twenty horrifying years, the war finally came to a conclusion.

The spirit of service to Mother Earth is also emphasized in hippie spirituality. Hippies regard the animals, trees, rivers, mountains, and sky as sacred (see tenet # 1). They believe that humans should devote considerable energy to protecting the one mother from which we all came from. Everything, then, from organizing a trash pick-up of a beloved park, to coordinating public campaigns against "development" projects, to peacefully resisting the construction of a massive petroleum pipeline on natural woodlands; captures every bit of the same spirit of service as helping a fellow human in need.

TENET 7: FREEDOM OF EXPRESSION CELEBRATED

Hippies have never been shy to freely express themselves. Personal expression can come through creative channels such as art, music, poetry, photography; or also through soulful activities like working the land or making love. Freedom of expression is the act of following the soul's desires. The Hippies' commitment to this principle is so unwavering, that they often find themselves in conflict over it with their family members-particularly parents and siblings. This tension emanates from a fear that loved ones have for the well-being of their (hippie) brethren. For in this society, the creative expressionist typically "dies" obscure and penniless. Or so we are told.

These family members attempt to herd their "lost" loved ones back onto the narrow-paved path of Dominant Society. Those who pressure their kin to abandon the hippie ethos have nothing but good intentions, though. This does not mean, however, that their actions are any less misguided. The appearance of this form of generational conflict reached a feverish pitch in the 1960's and continues today. In the current context, tensions are over the same issue: the right to freely set the course of one's own journey. Once more, hippies are demanding that others (particularly skeptical family and friends) respect this foundational freedom.

Finally, freedom of expression also implies an ability to worship in the manner they choose. If one views the Earth as sacred, he or she should be free to worship the trees and mountains without being criticized by others. Likewise, if some hippies choose to follow the dominant religion, they should be free to attend any Christian service they please, without being chastised by friends or family within the counterculture.

TENET 8: EMPHASIS ON ENERGY VIBRATIONS & BELIEF IN KARMA

Hippies believe that everything boils down to vibrations. The energy that we each put out to the Universe through our thoughts, intentions, and actions are highly charged and contribute to the shaping of the realities to which we all inhabit. We wind up creating environments when the energy vibrations of several beings merge together. Some can be dark and heavy while others become joyous and peaceful. Energy vibrations are the feelings of desperation that one feels while walking through an urban ghetto. They are also the intuitive knowing that all is one while on a walk in the woods. Many could agree that the woods more closely resemble the qualities of Godliness than the depressed city ghetto. For nature inspires faith and optimism, while the latter produces fear and dejection. So to say that something (or someone) has positive "vibes", is just another way of saying that it is more in tune with the spirit of Oneness. Vice versa. When one feels negative vibrations they are acknowledging a detached energy from the Creative Source.

Through becoming mindful of our own energy vibrations, hippies believe that positive environments can be cultivated. This means that one must learn to be conscious of their thoughts, intentions, and actions. As more come to do so, hippies are confident that the planet's collective consciousness will shift decidedly in the way of peace, unity, and love. Cultivating positive vibrations is not always easy, especially in this society. As a culture, we are too unaware of all that surrounds us to be mindful and too preoccupied with our own selfish pursuits to consider re-orienting (or establishing) our relationship with God. This is the point when the sacredness of the Earth (tenet 1), the practice of meditation (tenet 5), and freedom of expression (tenet 7) converge. The negative energy vibrations that one puts out can easily be converted into positive ones by simply spending time in nature, sitting in quiet, and finding a creative vehicle of expression.

Since hippies believe that everything relates back to energy vibrations, they also maintain that we can manifest our own destinies through directing energy (through our thoughts, intentions, and actions) to those outcomes that we desire. This phenomenon is sometimes called the "Laws of Attraction," but is really just another way of saying that our dreams can be realized through tapping in and flowing with the energies of the Universe. As we construct our own realities through the exercise of free will, it also means that our choices have energy vibrations attached to them.

The nature of these energy vibrations are called consequences. Generally speaking, hippies believe that the sum-total of all the types of consequences we have created (in the soul's eternal life) through our choices is called karma. If we have released more positive vibrations in the world through our thoughts, intentions, and actions than we are said to have "good karma." If we have done the opposite and put out mostly negative vibrations than we are said to have "bad karma". However, in reality, there is no such thing as having "good" or "bad" karma. For one's karmic state is never static or final. To be sure, there is definitely truth to the fact that what we call "good karma" is the build-up of those outcomes that more closely reflect godly qualities. Conversely, what we would label "bad karma" is the build-up of those outcomes that reflect the illusions of ego - our "hell".

The universe, then, can be thought of as a vast cosmic net. The nature of the energy vibrations that we put out to *IT* bounce back upon us in the forms of circumstances and events. It is these forms that comprise our "reality". As believers of karma, hippies would take issue with popular depictions of God as a wrathful deity. Rather, they would say, that we punish ourselves for the ungodly vibrations that we put out to the Cosmos. It is inspiring that the Great Mystery created a scheme so ingenious as to allow us to exact punishment upon ourselves. IT's motivations for doing so appear noble. It seems that the Universe wants us to learn from the consequence of choice. This implies that IT intended for all of us to evolve compassionately. It is equally inspiring that God made us co-creators in the unfolding of our own cosmic journeys.

TENET 9: GANJA AS A SACRED HERB

Admit it, you were wondering… when is he going to finally mention ganja? After all, you can't have hippies without it! While ganja is perfect for just about any setting or event, it holds a special place in the heart of hippie spirituality. Hippies have long acknowledged that the smoking of the mystical plant helps one turn inwards and reflect. Many are also aware that this sacred herb helps reveal truths into our personal relationships with God. Indeed, the divine properties of ganja are what separate it (aside from the fact it grows freely in nature) from manmade substances like alcohol, methamphetamines, and opiates. For whereas, the former fosters inner reflection and intuitive grounding, the latter substances help us escape from ourselves.

Hippies have long incorporated the smoking of ganja into their spiritual rites and traditions. Some of which include: walking in Mother Nature, meditation, yoga, writing, playing and listening to music, painting, sculpting, and dancing. Ganja is so revered in hippie circles, that The Farm made it a holy sacrament in the commune's earliest days. All other substances (including psychedelics) were banned. Ganja was signaled out for preferential treatment because these hippie pioneers acknowledged its deeper and divine purpose. As evidenced by the jailing of its late founder, Stephen Gaskin, for his role in the commune's past cultivation of herb, hippies have not always been free to openly express their love for this much maligned plant. This is because of Uncle Sam's outrageous and hypocritical "War on Drugs".

There is good news for hippies everywhere and it is that Ganja is now achieving widespread acceptance among the general public. Despite the US Government's 80-year campaign against marijuana users, several US states and municipalities are either legalizing the use of ganja for medicinal and or/recreational purposes, or decriminalizing its possession and use all together. In some places like Colorado, Oregon, and Washington DC, residents are even free to cultivate plants for personal use! More importantly, everyday people are coming to understand that ganja serves a significant function in some spiritual faiths.

TENET 10: ASPIRATIONS TO BUILD A SPIRITUAL COMMUNE
Deep down inside, all hippies share a common dream: to live off the land with fellow hippies in spiritual, self-sustaining communities. Some even make this dream a reality. The Farm is the best known example of one such community in the United States; but there are thousands of them scattered throughout the country. Communes are inspiring to hippies for at least five reasons:

- Communes offer people a space to practice their spiritual beliefs (relatively) free from the moral corruption of Dominant Culture
- The building of communes (in the countryside) affords hippies the opportunity to reestablish their roots in Mother Nature. Thus invigorating their lives with a sense of greater connection and purpose
- Living in a community gives hippies the chance to practice self-sufficiency. Learning how to provide for one's own food, water, and warmth is a revolutionary act in itself
- Spiritual communes serve as an inspiring example to others that people can live and work together in peace and harmony
- When members of spiritual communes join in collective action their impact on the world is both positive and inspiring. The Farm's humanitarian missions in Guatemala, Belize, and the Bronx are all cases in point

All of the above does beg one question: if building communes are a dream for so many hippies why don't more of them follow through on this desire? One obvious issue is money. To begin such a venture, hippies needs access to the very units of moral corruption that they devote much effort trying to detach from. Unfortunately, constructing the initial infrastructure of such an alternative society can be financially costly. One must first come up with the funds to purchase a large tract of land that is conducive to agriculture. Then there are the costs of building green technology to fuel the commune (rain collection tanks, solar panels, generators etc.), the cost of building shelters for people to live in (which can actually be affordable if built directly by the members of the commune), and the initial costs of healthcare provisions as the community transitions to one of self-reliance.

There also exists a second deterrent to hippies starting a commune, which is the belief that one's pursuit will ultimately fail. This concern stems from social conditioning that has us erroneously believe that it is impossible for a group of people to successfully drop out of society and live off the land. Of course, this line of pessimistic thinking is countered by the fact that there are at present over 4,000 communes in America! Many of which are wild success stories! Furthermore, no commune will ever fail if **All** of its members are united in faith in love.

*If you think I left out any key tenants of Hippie spiritualty off this list or you disagree with any of my descriptions with regard to the hippies' spiritual beliefs, practices, and aspirations feel free to leave a message post on the website: www.forrestrivers.com

And we can begin a dialogue.

Peace and Love,

Forrest Rivers

The Festival Drug Culture's Affront to Hippie Values

THE HIPPIE COUNTERCULTURE OF THE 1960's/70's, is best remembered for its challenges to conventional social norms and societal injustices. The Hippies were also well known for their soulful vehicles of creative and artistic expression, as well as being regarded for their unwavering message of peace, unity, and love. In the public's eye, the counterculture was also synonymous with the widespread use of mind altering drugs (like Acid) and visionary plants (like Magic Mushrooms and Peyote). To be sure, the experimentation with psychedelics can serve a noble purpose (see "Psychedelic Encounters with Spirit"). However, a growing drug culture -bearing the hippie label- has only proliferated since the heyday of the original hippies. Today, it is embodied in the current music festival circuit that grew out of THE "festival of all festivals", Woodstock. Unfortunately, many (but by no means all) people within this culture do not partake with the intent of gaining insight. Instead, hedonism is the order of the day.

THE FESTIVAL DRUG CULTURE

There is currently no better example of the perversion of hippie values than what is found in **mainstream** festival culture. To be sure, not all music festivals revolve around drugs. Irie Vibes, a reggae festival held in the Southeastern United States, embodies the hippie spirit just fine. Its attendees give great attention to the music and mostly refrain from using hard drugs and alcohol. There is plenty of ganja smoke in the air, but it is harmlessly used in conjunction with the music; it is not the lead act. The themes of peace, unity, and love are also reflected within each of the bands' music.

Many bluegrass and folk festivals are also known for their commitment to authentic hippie values. In the upstate town of Trumansville, New York, hippie folk gather annually at the Grassroots Festival of Music and Dance. The event is well known for both its inspiring cast of musicians and emphasis on community activism. One year that I attended, I saw several speakers come to the stage to lecture about hydro fracking. To my surprise, a group of festival goers gathered around to listen attentively. While the festival did have its fair share of psychedelics (which again, can be beneficial depending on one's intent), it did not have the vibe as somewhere people go just to use drugs.

The Burning Man culture is also seen by many festival goers as embodying hippie values. Once a year, "burners" from across the nation gather at an undisclosed location in the desert near Reno, Nevada. Over the course of a week (longer if one volunteers), participants erect their own town out of various art materials and establish tent stations that offer any vehicle of personal expression imaginable. Burning Man also emphasizes a "leave no trace" mentality. This means that participants agree to leave the desert as clean as they found it. The tradition of "gifting" is its most notable feature. Gifting refers to a form of economic exchange by which one party gives away any coveted resource (food, ganja, art work) to another. Crucially, the act is reinforced by one's willingness to give without receiving compensation in return. Gifting promotes the symbiotic values of unity and cooperation. At the conclusion of the festival, a giant handcrafted depiction of "The man", is burned down to the ground. The "Burn" is seen as a symbol of resistance to Dominant (commercial) Culture.

Burning Man and its smaller regional offshoots (called mini-burns) are the ostensible hippie's dream. After all, the festival appears to promote the values of freedom of expression (prominence of art), reverence for the natural world (leave no trace), and unity (gifting). To top it all off: the final denunciation of a corrupt and oppressive culture. Through attendance at two "mini-burns", however, I have personally found that rampant experimentation with the harder drugs like ecstasy, cocaine, and prescription medications are also common place among participants in the community. Among this group of people, the drugs still seem to be the emphasis. To be fair, the main event could turn out to be much different. One day soon I do hope to find out.

In contrast to the small group of festivals who promote hippie values, are those who appeal to the growing "hippie" drug sub culture. Over the course of the past half-decade, I have attended many such festivals. Some more than once. Within each, the use of hard drugs clearly prevailed over that of the hippie spirit. Below are brief descriptions of three of the most preposterous events that I have witnessed from these festivals. Each stood out for their brazen contradiction of what are thought of as hippie values.

Puppy For Sale

One year, at a festival in the Ozark Mountains of Arkansas, I was wandering around the festival grounds between sets. I was looking forward to watching a jam band that I had been waiting to see. As I made my way over to the stage, I came upon a man with dreadlocks and a beard. He was standing next to one of the vendor tables. I saw that he had a beautiful black lab puppy with him. As festival goers walked on by, this man offered to sell it for drugs. In stunned disbelief, I stopped in my tracks and shouted something to the effect of: "Yeah man, real hippie of you! Selling an animal just so you can get fucked up." This encounter led me to start questioning the authenticity of the festival culture. After all, the man dressed the part well: beard, dreadlocks, and sandals. A hippie he was not. Hippies display a reverence for all creatures. One does not prostitute a beloved animal so that they may fulfill their own hedonistic desires.

LEAVE NO TRACE

To their credit, most of the festivals that I have attended value the concept of "Leave no trace." Putting this principle into practice has proved difficult, though. At each one of the festivals, the grounds were defiled by the end. The participants at one particular gathering outside of Atlanta, Georgia, stood out for their blatant disregard for nature. Litter polluted the land by the end of the three-day event. Plastic water bottles were scattered across the beautiful landscape. Together, beer cans, cigarette butts, and food wrappers lined the ground with filth. It was appalling. Joining the pill popping/heavy psychedelic festival goers, were the college 'bro' or frat scene participants. The latter, I learned, have been attracted to music festivals by the electronic dub-step scene.

The mix of the two groups proved a volatile concoction. Aside from the eruption of some verbal altercations throughout the weekend, the natural surroundings suffered mightily. One night, when a trash can was no more than 10 feet away, I saw several drunk people throw their waste on the ground. When the trash cans were full, I watched several festival goers dump their trash into the woods behind the camp grounds. Despite organizers' best attempts to set up recycling bins, people still threw most of their plastic water bottles into the trash cans, thus restarting the vicious cycle. If people get so intoxicated that they cannot muster any reverence for their own Mother, what does that say about their capacity to respect one another?

A SCENE FROM HELL

One summer, my partner Rose and I, traveled a couple of hours from Nashville, Tennessee to watch our friends' reggae band (Roots of a Rebellion) perform at a festival. The band, who preaches an inspiring message of peace, love, and unity, played to a crowd of about 75 people. The two of us joined others who were grooving and dancing to the music. This festival was different. It was about the music and the forging of community…or so we thought. During ROAR's (as they are affectionately known) one hour set everyone was in good spirits. As people were smiling and dancing, I could feel the positive vibes. The band's music had clearly moved the crowd. However, at night, the scene shifted wildly.

Suddenly, everywhere I looked, there were drunk and strung out people. The scene deteriorated so badly that Rose and I retreated to our car. We wanted to avoid the boisterous yells and minor conflicts that engulfed the campground. While Rose went to sleep in the front seat, I decided to get out and explore. As I roamed, I saw two clearly strung out couples arguing. One couple was yelling about not having enough money to buy drugs. The other couple was bickering about having overpaid for them. The energy on the grounds felt uncomfortable.

As I began to make my way toward the music, I was approached by two fellow "festy" goers. I was asked if I wanted any "Zannies," (slang for a prescription drug) Molly, or Acid. I declined and continued. I walked over to the stage to observe the late night drug scene. Within minutes, I grew exceedingly uncomfortable. The musician playing in front of me was just as wasted as everyone else in the crowd. I scanned the small audience of about 35 people and recognized at least 10 faces who had been enjoying themselves (at my friends' show) earlier. They no longer seemed to be having fun. I looked down by my feet and saw one girl slouched down on the ground with her head between her knees. These once vibrant people had morphed into mindless zombies.

Explanations for the Drug Sub Culture

The public's identification of hippies with this festival drug subculture is unfortunate. Rather than being viewed as spiritual advocates for the planet and humanity (which true hippies are), they are dismissed as hedonistic drug addicts trying to escape from "reality." These perceptions come with disastrous consequences. The human race is in desperate need of unity. The alienation of more conformist minded folk (the majority of people) from the peaceful mindset of hippies, amounts to a missed encounter at this coming together.

Aside from fostering more separation, the distorted image of the hippie also plays right into the hands of our cultural managers. This elite group, fears the hippies' message of liberation and love. The most influential segments of this power block, include the structures of church, state, and corporation. It is plain to see why the purveyors of Dominant Culture despise the hippie: because they openly criticize and offer soulful alternatives to those institutions that feed humanity's grand illusion. As long as hippies and the drug culture remain locked in the publics' mind, elites will continue to find success in playing the people off one another.

One's participation in this drug subculture also has the effect of alienating the festival goer from their inner self, the essence of who they truly are. To be sure, many participants are (to some degree) seeking a deeper connection with spirit. The problem arises when they fail to ground this yearning in soulful practices. However, like the leashed dog who craves its freedom, one's natural impulse to connect can be stymied by external controls. A familiar example of such an impediment is found through participation in a consumer-driven economy which forces one to give up their personal autonomy and sell their labor for mediocre wages. This type of work is often described as "soul crushing".

Organized religion may also (ironically) disrupt one's desire to connect. The church is assumed by many people to be a place of spiritual communion, yet it's self-righteous and fear provoking ways are great adversaries to divine experience. With so many people drawn into its sphere of influence, it is not surprising that disillusionment results on a mass scale. Viewed in this light, it becomes clearer why people in the drug subculture turn to substance abuse in the first place: to simultaneously withdraw from the many indignities of day to day life while attempting to foster a genuine connection in place of the absence of one. To be sure, one's sense of alienation feeds the drug culture, but each individual also makes the conscious choice to partake in it. The fact that it exists also reflects a great misunderstanding on its participants' parts of how to consciously exercise free will. When is one said to exercise free will in a conscious manner? When a person's thoughts, intentions, and actions align to represent the spirit of Oneness. Reflecting on the exercise of personal freedom, the late writer and activist, Stephen Gaskin, said the following:

> *"The only freedom man has comes through responsibility. And responsibility means not only doing what is right for yourself in any situation—but also by what is right for others".*

Confusion as to its nature unfortunately abounds in a society that emphasizes self-aggrandizement over concern for more enriching pursuits. The identification of hippies with the festival drug culture is best described as a tragedy. So, it is the duty of everyone who identifies with the authentic hippie spirit to point out the hypocrisies within the festival circuit. In so doing, however, one must also practice compassion. Like the rest of us, they too, are searching for a connection with Oneness.

INFUSING HIPPIE VALUES INTO THE FESTIVAL CULTURE

Something must be done to redefine the purpose why people attend these festivals. In so long as participants associate the circuit with wanton displays of debauchery, an emphasis on hippie values will continue to take a backseat. Every effort should be made, then, to make the festival a more spiritually enriching experience. Of course, this responsibility first falls on the shoulders of festival organizers. The task of drawing more conscience-minded musicians might mean dropping acts from the Electronic Dance Music (EDM) scene. One might fill reggae, bluegrass, and folk artists in their place.

Ultimately, though, the performers must accept responsibility for injecting more uplifting music into festivals. Musicians need to be more conscious of what venues they accept to play, and remember that it is they who drive the demand for these musical gatherings in the first place. The festival goers (ostensibly) attend these events for the music. If the music doesn't tune them in, they turn on to drugs. In the course of exercising more discretion on what venues to play, musicians may find that they have to turn down more lucrative offers. Obviously, this can present a difficult situation for those independent bands who find themselves in rough financial waters. The responsibility also falls on the financial support of fans to ensure that conscious musical acts can continue to make and play music.

Closer coordination between independent organizers, musicians, and their fans is also a necessary component in creating a more spiritually enriching festival experience. For example, organizers could invite various practitioners from the local community (such as a meditation instructor) to teach their techniques to the group. Then, the following day, a speaker, writer, or activist could come and impart his/her knowledge. Why not also block off a few times during the day for poetry readings or mini art shows? Another way to promote a more enriching festival experience, is to greater emphasize the natural surroundings on which they are commonly held. Of the many festivals I attended, a good majority were held in pristine wilderness areas. Perhaps, event coordinators could set up short group hikes throughout the day. This, too, would ignite authentic connection.

Crucially, the task of infusing these events with hippie values falls on the festival goers themselves. Would be participants need to ask themselves this important question before making the decision to attend: what is my purpose for going? If one's sole reason is to use drugs, stay home. The planet is already too saturated with aimless and chaotic energy. If your intention is to enjoy inspiring music while connecting with yourself and others... then more power to you!

Of course, it may turn out to be that some of the attendees are unwilling to turn inwards and reflect upon their true intentions. If that is the case, it may be high time to rethink the entire notion of a festival. In such an instance, it would be up to all of us to educate would be attendees about the pitfalls of festival culture; and to point out that many of its devotees are really wolves dressed in hippie sheep clothing.

Poetry and Reflections from Inspiring Folk

WRITINGS BY ALEX C.

Otsego Song

A low, heavy fog fills the voids of the valley's rolling hills,
And winds roil up rolling waves on green waters.
Fluffy ducklings scuttle and chase one-another for fresh-caught crayfish,
And mother duck watches over, gazing lake-ward on cresting, shore-bound waves.
Ten-man-tall Willow weeps its ancient sorrow into soothing waters,
Soft breezes caress her long tendrils of blue-green and gold,
Leaves dip and ripple and this echoes through the hearts of ducklings and me,
Our Oneness stripped bare, our true selves revealed, our pains accepted and forgotten.
Westward falls the sun as shadows climb the eastern hills,
All our souls to follow in swift succession,
Till the morning comes and lights the chambers of our hearts,
For which the Great Waves roll forever.

All called Away, Together:

The mountains, they call my name.
I hear whispered words on winter winds.

They've come over foothills and across plains.
Traveled lakes' expanses and ridden rusty railroad.
Cries resonate and echo in my heart and make music in the mazes of my mind.
Taken slowly, writing two histories into one.
Whatever comes now, in the momentous crescendo of my entangled soul,
Time takes it now into the Passing.
Into the cries that cling,
To the shimmering reflections of all others.

WRITINGS BY SEAN MURPHY

Untitled

As I stand here, lying among fellow pawns..
An impulse flashes through my consciousness.
When can I fly?
When can I caress the treetops with my wings?
When can I speak across the mountains and hear them whisper back?
...As I meander in a bliss up the mountain side
I ask myself transformed, inspired,
Intoxicated by the smears of autumn encroaching upon the valleys,
I remember...
Wondering how i could forget, when?
Blowing the sun a kiss into the moonlight,
soaring to heights long forgotten...
I remember.

A Peaceful Bliss

True and honest, you live by my side
A passion, love and beauty you don't know how to hide
My friend and comrade we share our lives
A peaceful Bliss you present upon all

Except those of whom are hunted by the primal side
Smiling triumphantly at life you lift my heart
Snuggled by my side you lift my soul
A fury noble wisdom,
An unwavering peace,
An unconditional love
My dearest

POEM BY AUSTIN SMITH

Untitled

Just an artist and His stencil,
Trying to simplify thoughts with paper and pencil,
For each time I cry, I pray it's followed with a sigh,
Of relief and belief that at LEAST it feels good to be alive,
And through THIS revelation and constant meditation,
A child within is reborn, again and again…
Through **Faith**, **Work**, and **Love** alone,
Will I achieve salvation of my own,
My only wish is one you know:
I want to steadily grow,
Each of us though,
Into the individuals we DREAM to know,
Just as pillars of the temple stand apart,
I too want to save room for our own heart,
For all of life's twists and turns may help to bloom,
Into grateful mindfulness morning, night and noon
Dear Lord, please let me be the change I want to see,
Help me heed the wise words of the great minds of history,
Not worry, not fear, not be anywhere but here,
Right now,
For time IS running out,

And every moment we're choosing our own route,
Whether we like it or not...

WRITINGS BY ROSE

Mother Water
The waterfall shapes the mountainside
through its winding streams,
providing for all it touches.
The journey down the hillside greets the water
with the mouths of worthy spirits,
and the trees searching for the sun...
nuzzling their roots around the rocks
for their earthly grounding;
forever kissed by the flowing stream.
It touches all beings with tenderness and care,
unifying all of absolute being
to the gentle vibrations transmitted and received.
The water worries not of time,
Nor do the rocks or trees- they just Are.
No hurry to become as there is no rush to live...
we will forget the temporal sensations as the water cleanses,
inviting you in with all of its being.
Traveling forward but ever present with each moment it encounters,
carrying the memory of its past but awakening even n o w.
Feel the water rush over you;
join its blessed call to the universe.

Untitled
Amongst the cities you will find the bustling waves of people passing
in hurried rhythms to clocks racing no end.
But head past the pavement and soar to lands untouched,

with roaring streams along enchanted hillsides you will find true stillness.
In silence all doors will be opened and walls dismantled,
with the soul's wishes all illusion dissolves
in the bliss that is the trees, rocks, and riverbeds.
Go inward to hear the call of your truth
guiding the virtues of your subtle being,
freedoms released in the winds
that dance around your head unite all of existence to one.
Encountering sacred footsteps with quiet minds, the spirits come alive…
give host to your soul for its time is everlasting.

Untitled

Existing in the infinite limitations of your own reality.
seeking shelter forming concepts that echo of past,
but how to let the soul wander I say…
and feel to ease its conscious actions wrapped in love-
to treat each day a new. We greatly find to each his own
and in turn a divinely bound web of light to be in all.
Temporary incarnations of becoming to wisdom not found through
subtle reasons but rather through deep intuitive knowing,
hush now you are that **Eternal Child of Love.**

Earth Spirit

Breathe in the tranquil energy of Love flowering itself
found in the sanctuary of the hillside,
all life flows to the heartbeat of Mother Earth,
so we've come to sing a joyous tune of remembrance
and to the beauty of existence in one's current breath-
the deer trusts in its heart, as you should too.
all found too soon is a call to the spirit;
peace so easy…
the sun brings all its children home,
granting permission with a smile.

The everlasting waves of the universe are with you,
as is all of time.
So trust in your footsteps
and trust in your knowing,
for your soul will never forsake you.
The soul is universal, the soul is pure.
Your spirit, your being;
united in all, rooted in Love.
Ignited from the heart's fire within
spread to all brothers and sisters of the universe...
oh how we are Infinitely One.

The Spiritual Revolution Will Not Be Televised

THE WESTERN WORLD IS SUBMERGED in the darkest depths of ego. The exploitation of the natural world, wars of aggression, and the suppression of Indigenous cultures via "globalization" are all examples. Much of the west is sickened by a spiritual disease that has become a global pandemic. Too many people are motivated by nothing more than monetary gain, status, and fame. Still, others are so lost in their narcissistic worlds of impersonal technologies like Facebook, cell phones, video games, and iPads, that they are rendered incapable of sustaining human interactions.

Furthermore, we live in a society where our government leaders commit (increasingly) brazen acts of cruelty against people across the globe, lie to its citizens on a regular basis, and make active preparations to use force against their own brothers and sisters for raising their voices in protest. From that foolish farce that we call money, we have created and helped steer the transfer of nature's precious resources into the hands of a few private individuals and corporations. All the while, many live and suffer in dire poverty.

Organized religion has been unable to provide a spiritual road map through this labyrinth of moral decay. Younger generations are coming to regard church authorities with greater suspicion and, given their countless scandals, rightly so. Unfortunately, far too many of us exchange the God of fear and control for that of reason and logic, bypassing all together the life source of spirit. Despite the sad state of our world, we must not have fear for our future for two reasons: first, the very miracle that is life should fill us all with great hope. Isn't it remarkable enough that we are even here? It is also incredible that we are able to experience love and communicate our joy and sorrow with one another. This is all evidence of a presence far greater then ourselves. How then, can we possibly fear what we have not yet come to know?

Secondly, we are now embarking upon a great period of spiritual transformation. This inner progression of our species, will likely unfold over the course of the next hundred years. Over that time, changes will be so dramatic that we will hardly recognize our current way of being. We can expect to see a return back to the age-old forms of tribal living that still persists in many parts of the world. In addition, we will transition from global economies in favor of scaling back down to local markets of trade and barter. Government, as we understand it, will cease to exist. All such matters will be handled directly by the people. Having realized the great harm done to the planet, we will honor and worship the Earth. Great care will be taken to make sure we only extract what we need from the planet. A genuine commitment to the principles of sustainability will prevail. With our human family united around the ends of peace, war will become a relic of the past.

The above description is our ultimate fate, but there are many people who are not yet aware that society is in desperate need of a revolution. This is due to an extensive web of social conditioning that begins in childhood. While the majority of the people are not tuned into the moment, it doesn't mean they won't become so. We must remember that it is our collective destiny to awaken. The first step of this awakening is for each of us to identify the egoistic values that currently guide our thoughts, intentions, and actions. This is how we will begin to liberate ourselves from the illusion.

The following writing is broken down into three parts:

* Part 1 describes the guiding egoistic values that underlie our current social conditioning and how they structure our individual and collective states of unconsciousness

- Part 2 outlines the new inspiring values that will come to inform the age of the spiritual revolution
- Part 3 breaks down into three sections and offers my personal perspectives on how the spiritual revolution might unfold

Part One: The Worship of Ego

Consider each of the following scenarios:

Tom

Growing up, Tom was taught that competition was a natural state for man. In elementary school, his teachers emphasized the close biological links between the ultra-competitive chimpanzees and humans. They glossed over the even closer ties between man and the highly cooperative Bonobo monkeys. His teachers also provided small rewards (such as candy or stickers) to the student(s) who answered questions correctly. Like any child, Tom enjoyed the praise he received for a job well done, but he also derived satisfaction from being the first to answer the question. At home, Tom's parents reinforced his emerging competitive drive. They pushed him into organized sports like basketball, pee wee football, and baseball. However, his parents' emphasis was not on the cooperative/team work aspects of these activities. His mother, a businesswoman, wanted her son to learn how to be assertive, and she thought sports a good avenue for this. His Father, a doctor, wanted him to learn the value of structure, a prerequisite for commercial success.

As it would turn out, Tom became accomplished in each of the three sports. In high school, he went on to captain the varsity baseball and football teams. Aside from learning tremendous self-discipline, Tom most enjoyed the high he got from winning and the prestige that followed. In high school, he liked that everyone seemed to know his name. He especially enjoyed the attention from girls! Tom's social conditioning continued inside the classroom as well. For example, in his biology classes, he learned about Charles Darwin's theory of natural selection and its central role in our evolutionary development. Darwin's perspectives seemed to match up with his own.

Tom began to apply the notion of the "survival of the fittest" to an understanding of his own athletic prowess. Tom was never taught that there existed alternative interpretations of evolutionary theory. His teachers glossed over the equally plausible theory of evolution put forth by such biologists as Peter Kropotkin, who spent considerable time studying and writing about the cooperative nature of ants, and found that cooperation plays a prominent role in all species' evolutionary progression. Tom's history and social studies' teachers only reinforced the competition narrative. Both failed to emphasize the successful social models (centered around cooperation) of the Indigenous cultures of the world. Nor, did his teachers clarify the links between the ascent of his own culture, the principle of competition, and the genocide of the Native populations.

At home, Tom's parents continued to push him in his athletic pursuits. It paid off. He received a full scholarship to play both baseball and football at a prestigious college. Once he enrolled at the university, Tom continued his dominance in sports—even attracting the eye of some minor league baseball scouts. His competitive drive, however, began to extend into each and every aspect of his life. He constantly saw himself in openly petty contests with his friends and peers. Ultimately, Tom would go on to earn a Bachelor's degree in business and marketing. In his first few years after graduation, Tom worked in two marketing positions before landing a sales job at a major fortune 500 company called Monsanto. Over the course of the next decade, Tom catapulted himself up the hierarchy of the monster biotechnology firm. With his competitive instincts freshly sharpened, he climbed his way into a high level Vice President post. There, he would go on to manage the corporation's controversial Genetically Modified Organisms (GMO) project.

Prior to accepting the post, Tom had learned of the moral dilemmas surrounding the genetic alteration of the food supply: the strong association with cancer, the economic ruin visited upon small farmers and poor nations, as well as animal cruelty. As Tom thought about the benefits of the job (relative job security and a handsome salary of $ 350,000 with stock options) he couldn't turn it down. Years passed, and Tom grew comfortable in his new role. As company profits from GMO's soared, so too did his salary. By the end of his fifth year on the job, Tom was earning upwards of $ 6 million per year. But Tom's salary wasn't the only thing that soared. Cancer rates among the public (due in no small part to GMO's) continued to climb to record highs, as did the number of small family farm foreclosures. Time went on and Tom even learned of the company's ignoble past with Agent Orange—a highly toxic chemical. Tom chose to look the other way. He did not want to face the collective maladies that his company visited upon humanity. He had risen to the top of the corporate hierarchy and with all the material perks befit of a man of his status: big house(s), vacation properties, political influence (Tom later went on to serve as an adviser to the FDA) and relative fame. Tom had more than "made it," and that is all that mattered to him.

NICOLE

As a child, Nicole's parents always taught her that people could not be trusted. To support this perspective, they spoke of the great horrors reported on the television news. Nicole also grew up in a strict Catholic household, so the theme of fear was reinforced in mass every week. The Priest would remind the congregation that they were all naturally "sinners" and that the Lord Jesus Christ had died on the cross to absolve them of sin. He would then spend much of his sermon specifying the copious ways in which they upset God before prescribing a series of rituals to avoid damnation. Discussion of matters like sin and hell are sure to arouse great apprehension in any child.

Throughout Nicole's adolescent years, her distrust of people was reinforced by her teachers. One day, she asked her humanities instructor why people commit violence against one another. The teacher responded, "it is in our nature to do evil. We naturally want what the other person has. That is why we need government." It didn't dawn on Nicole that her teacher had made this claim without addressing the(relatively) peaceful states of most indigenous cultures prior to European Colonization. Her explanation of human nature rested on the dubious myth of competition.

After high school, Nicole enrolled at a local community college to major in criminal justice. Convinced of man's inherently cruel nature, she would study to work in law enforcement. As a police officer, Nicole reasoned, she could help protect people from one another. Her draw to the matters of "law and order", was a reflection of her own social conditioning. At the time that Nicole completed her criminal justice degree, she graduated from the police academy. Over the course of the next 25 years she would go on to enjoy a celebrated career in law enforcement. During her tenure, Nicole rose steadily through the ranks. She even finished out her career as a chief narcotics official for the Federal Government. In this capacity, she helped facilitate the country's campaign against drug users. Her specialty was in the area of marijuana enforcement. In this role, Nicole was personally involved in several counter-drug operations. On the surface, the stings appeared righteous. After all, she was helping keep dope off the streets! In reality, this campaign revealed a dark side.

In one instance, Nicole ordered raids on a number of neighboring medical marijuana dispensaries in California. Despite obtaining legal standing under state law, she carried out the government's assertion of federal power anyways. In so doing, Nicole dispatched over a hundred armed-SWAT team members to the various locations. As a result, all 11 of the dispensaries were forcibly shut down and its owners were arrested for violation of federal laws. Several employees of the dispensaries were also arrested and charged with petty drug offenses. Unfortunately, the raids only increased the suffering of those patients who required access to the medicinal cannabis. Absent the herb, many of these same patients (some of who suffered with diseases like cancer) would be forced to go back on highly addictive prescription drugs.

Throughout her tenure in drug enforcement, Nicole was also involved in several other moral quandaries, including her department's "mistaken" killing of two unarmed men believed to be associated with a Drug Cartel; to allegations that her own agency helped shield the Central Intelligence Agency (CIA) from their own local drug operations. The actions of her own office also raised questions about the overall growth of police power within the nation. Was Nicole aware that she might be contributing to both repression and suffering at home?

Up until her very last days on the "Force", Nicole maintained that man could not be trusted. Rather, if left to their own devices, humans would visit great indignities upon one another. Nicole saw her work as virtuous. She was keeping the "bad guys" off the street.

GREG

As the son of two military veterans, Greg was raised in a strict household. While not quite crossing into physical abuse, discipline was both swift and severe. One time Greg's parents discovered that their nine-year-old son had stolen a pack of gum. As a punishment, they forced him to stand in the corner of a room for two hours straight. Another time, Greg was grounded for two weeks for earning a "B" in one of his middle school classes. It went without saying, that he was expected to earn all "A's". Greg's time spent with friends was also closely monitored, and his parents forbade him from dating until he was eighteen years old. It was also expected of their son to display a love of his country. In fact, one of his parents' fondest sayings was: "My country, right or wrong."

Having been conditioned to fight in war, Greg's parents had a very black and white narrative of the world. They both believed in the presence of a higher power, but their conceptions of divinity reflected a dualistic world divided between "good" and "evil". Those "fighting" on the side of "virtue" included: the patriots who fought and died for their nation, the officers who uphold "law and order", and those God fearing Christians who earned a living from the sweat off their brow. Those erring on the side of the "wicked" included: the sworn "enemies" of America, the dirty long haired "freaks" who questioned authority, and any religious belief that ran counter to Christianity.

Overtime, Greg came to adopt a similar world view as his parents. This perspective further blossomed, after he was sent away to a Christian college. It was there when Greg took a keen interest in the Church's interpretation of scripture and decided that he would be a preacher. Upon his graduation, he enrolled in a graduate program and earned a degree in theology. When he completed his academic work, he went on to become a Baptist minister at a conservative local perish. With a gaggle of followers, Greg began to spread his influence to others. Aside from his day to day preaching, he wrote two notable books that attracted the attention of the Christian Broadcasting Network (CBC)—a media outlet for the dissemination of fundamentalist Christian beliefs. The CBC contacted Greg and offered him a weekly television show to deliver his perspectives to viewers. He readily accepted and officially became a televangelist.

Now known for his charismatic delivery and fiery rhetoric, Greg launched into his beliefs about God. First and foremost, God was made in the image of man and imbued with masculine qualities. "HE" was a wrathful deity who delivered vengeance upon all non-Christians. As a supreme note-taker of sorts, "HE" kept track of each sin that one committed. As for those poor souls who didn't accept Jesus in their life (as conceived by the church) a fearful fate awaited them in the form of hell. On his program, Greg listed homosexuals, feminists, "Islamic radicals" (not appreciating the irony) and "tree hugging" hippies as the worst sinners of all. According to Greg, these groups represented the height of man's depravity.

Sometimes, Greg would even launch into tirades against one of these groups. In the weeks after the September 11th terrorist attacks, he spoke for 40 minutes about the "evil" of Islam and its violent culture. Conveniently, Greg failed to make mention of the equally gruesome acts perpetrated by the charlatans of his own faith like the Crusades, the missionary campaigns to "Christianize" Indigenous populations, as well as acts of terrorism carried out against doctors who perform abortions. His views on humans' relationship to nature was simple: the earth was put here for our sole fulfillment. Thus, the extraction of its resources were seen as a divine right. The notion of life as an interconnected web was a concept that Greg bypassed all together. The egoistic expression of separateness emerged as the common theme in each of Greg's sermons. His world outlook was hatched from the fear he encountered in childhood. The idea of God as a radiant source of unconditional love was also a concept foreign to Greg.

ANITA

As far back as she could remember, Anita's parents spoke of the great accomplishments of western culture. Her mom was a chemist and her dad a math teacher. Together, they emphasized the West's technological advancements in modern medicine, but overlooked social problems such as our society's staggering rates of cancer and high drug addiction rates. When speaking of society's strengths, Anita's parents spoke of the mass availability of convenient consumer products but they said nothing about the impact consumerism had on the natural world. They gushed on about the numerous benefits of the information age, but glossed over its potential negative effects as well. Her parents' devotion to reason pushed them away from organized religion while their intellectual self-righteousness blocked their spiritual paths. For Anita's parents, science was their God, and they both waved its flag of "progress" with great vigor. From their perspective, the West's technological innovations placed their society "head and shoulders" above the rest.

As Anita made her way through school, the theme of "progress" was brought up again and again. Her history teachers cast western culture in a highly favorable light. When recounting the past, they emphasized the ties between the West's staggering economic wealth and its scientific/technological advances. These same teachers spoke approvingly of the West's right to expand into the territories of indigenous societies on the grounds that they were "civilizing" their cultures. Curiously, Anita's mentors also sugarcoated the mass genocide that this crusade for "progress" inflicted upon the people of the Earth.

Infatuated by the theme of progress in Western culture, Anita went on to college, where she earned a PhD in history. After completing her advanced degree, she accepted a faculty position at a prestigious research university. Once there, Anita would go on to pen several popular academic books on the West. Eventually, she became so renowned in her field that she won a coveted grant from a western heritage foundation. Her task: to write a college textbook on Western Civilization from the year 1650 to the present day. Ecstatic, she accepted the grant, and began work on the ambitious project. Anita would finish the book in only three years.

In her textbook (which would eventually reach thousands on both sides of the Atlantic) she made four academic assumptions:

* The west is a "unique" and "advanced" culture for its scientific and technological breakthroughs
* The natural world was a key "backdrop" in the West's ascent
* Despite some "minor disruptions" Industrialization was still a positive development for the human race
* The West's high standard of material living outfitted its citizens with the greatest availability of "freedom" in the world

The book's themes reinforced the concept of western cultural supremacy. From a spiritual perspective, Anita fell into the egoistic trappings of separateness. In her emphasis on the "uniqueness" and "advancement" of western culture, she failed to speak truth to the reality that...**we are all one.** Now reaching a wide-spread audience, Anita's textbook was as notable for what it omitted, as it was for its cultural distortions (see above). For example, only in passing did the author address the mass genocide of the Native population, which came to characterize much of western expansion. In fact, Anita drew little attention to how western nations acquired the land needed for expansion in the first place. Other than an admission of its regrettable nature, Anita also glossed over the prominent role that slavery played in the West's initial "development." When discussing the theme of religion and society in the United States, she made little reference to the long established spiritual beliefs of the Natives—whose God is found in the sacredness of nature.

From a broader perspective, the book's biggest flaw was in its inability to expand the definition of the term "progress". For example, a Buddhist monk would have had a much different interpretation of what "progress" entailed than a scientist. More than likely, the monastic being would associate the phrase with one's spiritual path. Despite its blatant distortions, glaring omissions, and general undertone of ethnocentrism, the text went on to become a best-seller. While the price of the textbook soared in monetary value, another price was exacted on its many readers... ignorance.

FOUR SCENARIOS, ONE EGOISTIC VISION:
Taken together, the negative qualities of competition, fear, separateness, and ignorance form the bedrock of western culture. Through our families, schools, governments, and churches we are all (subtly) conditioned to practice these values. Thus, as each of us come to be detached from our true essence, we wind up with some of the collective problems described above. What the times call for is a true spiritual revolution. One in which we replace each of the egoistic attributes with spiritual ones. In place of competition we need cooperation. Instead of fear we must cultivate faith. Finally, we need unity as a substitute for separateness. Each of these new values must be shepherded by truth, the great light of love.

The laying down of this spiritual framework will help end our personal and collective suffering. It will also address what even the most noble and dedicated social reformers have not: the problem of ego. Rather than treat the symptoms of the disease (as we have tried to do through social activism), we need to strike at the root of our suffering. It is our destiny to make this quantum leap in consciousness.

PART II: THE FOUR GUIDING VALUES OF THE SPIRITUAL REVOLUTION
Below are descriptions of four values that will come to guide mankind's spiritual awakening.

COOPERATION

Cooperation is any act of reciprocity shared between two or more beings. In a cooperative relationship both (or more) parties directly benefit from the action(s) of the other(s). In nature, we see examples of this quality. Take the interaction between a flower and a bee. The dynamics of their partnership are mutually beneficial. The flower receives the gift of life through the bee's pollination, and the bee sustains itself through the flower's sweet nectar. Crucially, neither of the two beings benefit at the expense of the other.

Cooperation can also be thought of as a key building block of our existence. Its qualities transcend all aspects of our reality. Just as cooperation is present in the symbiotic relationship of the brain to the heart, so it is cosmically, between our soul and the physical body. Each finds their expression in the other. Cooperation also channels the divine through its emphasis on equality. For in such an exchange, the concerns and interests of both (or more) parties are fully satisfied. True equality lends meaning to the concept of oneness.

As we evolve spiritually, cooperation will gradually come to supplant competition as one of our core foundational values. Finished will be the bloody turf wars over money. No longer will we engage in petty contests over fame and status. Only through cooperation can we honor the inner essence of all life forms.

Faith

True faith is to trust in the very essence of self
It is the knowing of a presence infinitely divine
Faith transcends all our configurations of time
And as that is its way, it fears not for today
For how can one despair in moments
That are cosmically eternal?
Faith is to extend compassion to all beings
Even to those who have wronged you
Faith is a feeling that overwhelms one

On a walk into nature
Faith when it is applied inspires
The discovery of a lifelong passion
Faith is about finding hope in a brighter future
And the promise
Of a better world that reflects our divineness
Faith does not acknowledge dogma
It is pure as gold and comprised of:
Unconditional Love.

UNITY

Unity is a collective awareness that we are all children of god. It is about the breaking down of all forms of classification among mankind, and between man and all living beings. Unity is a prerequisite to the achievement of peace. Following the spiritual revolution, the various seeds of disunity will dissipate, as we come to see that each of our present divisions are merely constructs of the ego.

UNITY CONTINUED: AN EXERCISE

Think of and feel these sources of conflict that divide the human race: religious, socio-economic, gender, racial, ethnic, and national. Now, identify at least one example of each source of separation. What did you come up with? For an example of religious division, you may have thought of the ongoing conflict between Christians and Muslims that has proliferated since the terrorist attacks of September 11th, 2001. For an instance of socioeconomic division, you may have noted the schism that exists between wealthy corporations and the working class, best captured by the eruptions of the Occupy Wall Street protests in 2011 and Democracy Spring in 2016. For an illustration of gender division you may have drawn on the persistent pay gap between men and women, or worse, the disturbing rates of sexual assault committed against females.

Racial division may have brought up horrible memories of black children being sprayed by fire hoses during the Civil Rights movement, or the rash of modern-day police shootings perpetrated against African-Americans. Ethnic division may engender disturbing images of the Palestinian/Israel conflict. Finally, for national division, you may have pointed to the countless atrocities of war and genocide committed by governments worldwide.

Next, try to describe the philosophical assumptions underlying each form of disunity. What did you come up with? The premise underlying religious division is that it is righteous to defend the "one" true path way to God. The assumptions driving socioeconomic division are that the separation of the people into "rich" and "poor", are justified because individuals have different talents and abilities. The ideological framework driving gender and racial division (respectively) rests on bigoted theories of inferiority. Namely, that women and non-whites are somehow intended (by God) to be something lesser than their male and white counterparts. Ethnic division is implicitly justified on the grounds that alternative cultures pose a "threat" to one's own. Finally, "statesmen" contend that conflict between nations is natural on account that the "good" nations have a moral obligation to vanquish the "evil" ones.

Now examine each of these assumptions. Do you see any moral dilemmas in any or all of them? What did you find? To begin with, how can there only be one true path way to God? Have those so personally met God? Or are they merely saying what they think IT would believe? Another possibility exists all together: What if God's love is unconditional and there are numerous pathways to connect? Viewed in this light, the worship of nature (as practiced by many Indigenous cultures) is no less divine than the Christians' worship of Jesus Christ. Rather than being divided, both groups share the common ground of believing in a higher source and living a righteous life. These similarities should be emphasized.

Fallacies also exist with the justification of social classes. It is true, that people are born with varied talents and abilities; but do they necessarily have to be expressed as rich and poor? For example, most tribal cultures, globally, have maintained (relatively) egalitarian social structures. In fact, great inequities of wealth are shunned upon in their societies. A culture's choice to introduce competition into their society, is what results in the division of the two groups. Economic inequality is not a given or "natural" phenomenon. Additionally, the problem of money also undermines the social constructs of rich and poor. Money isn't real. It is an illusionary unit of value that we assign to coveted goods extracted from nature.

There are also flaws in the ignorant assumptions of both sexism and racism. How do we know that men and white people are superior? Who decided that this was so? A wealthy, white male? Finally, where did the criteria of this supposed superiority derive from? Surely, they did not obtain it from God! Why would the Eternal One differentiate humans on account of such superficial aspects as one's gender and racial make-ups?

Just as baseless are the moral justifications for ethnic division. Do other cultures really pose a threat to one's own? Or, are there transcendent qualities of existence that bind all cultures of the world together? For example, we all share in our need to find a plentiful and clean water source to survive. So, too, must we all cultivate nutritious foods and find shelter. All peoples of the world crave peace and serenity in their lives. War between ethnic groups is not a natural state for man, either. We were all put here to experience something greater than the egoistic hatreds of the physical world. Maybe all ethnic cultures can unite around the fact that we are all children of the mystical Universe.

Finally, are not nations, too, a fictitious construct of the human mind? As well as a card to be played in the pursuit of power by ambitious men and women? How many of us even had a say in the forging together of America? The Native Americans? Blacks? Women? The Farmers? How can a nation be "good" or "evil"? Aren't such perceptions in the eye of the beholder? The United States views "herself" as fighting on behalf of what is righteous. However, throughout much of the world, "she" is regarded as the greatest threat to world peace by our brothers and sisters. Does this constitute the United States as evil? We will never achieve unity until we stop seeing the world as separate. We are all one.

TRUTH

There are four universal truths. These exist cosmically and point to our existential nature. As for the meaning of "truth," there is only one: truth is subjective.

THE FOUR UNIVERSAL TRUTHS

Universal Truth One: Existence of Higher Planes of Consciousness

Our physical bodies are merely temporary hosts for our soul. When our body dies, our conscious essence goes on to somewhere else. Just where its goes remains one of the great mysteries of life. Through the meditative visions of many Yogis', and through copious research gathered through hypnotic, past life regressions and near death experiences (NDE's), it would appear that the soul lives on, even as the body dies. The presence of an afterlife would imply that there are higher spiritual planes we transcend into after the physical life/death cycle. The belief in this afterlife is universally accepted as truth by all religious/spiritual faiths.

Universal Truth Two: Existence of a Higher Power

Many people call *IT* "God", while others, "The Great Mystery". Some descriptions are of an all knowing "Presence". Perhaps, it could be referred to as the "Eternal One". Whatever one prefers to name it, IT's very essence cannot be defined. Those who try to enforce characteristics onto IT risk casting their own biases onto that which defies description. This is how we end up with religious dogma. God (or however you choose to call the being responsible for creation) means different things to different people. There are multiple ways to connect to IT.

While God cannot be defined, nor can IT's presence be denied. How can something as miraculous as life, be explained away as mere "chance" or "coincidence?" This computer, which I am writing on, didn't just one day become a machine. It was assembled using human brains and hands. It had a creator then. The same idea, applies to the gases and molecules that scientists say we evolved from. What, or who, created these molecular compounds? Can something spring from nothing? If so, them how? These molecular compounds were the work of a glorious artist, with a divine plan. Those who devote time trying to prove God's absence, strip the wonder from their own lives.

Universal Truth Three: Union of Suffering and Joy

In the West, suffering and joy are often expressed as polar opposites. This is not necessarily so as both suffering and joy are interconnected. In fact, one cannot experience true bliss without first navigating through the pain and sorrow that proceeded it. To be with suffering is to also strengthen one's inner resolve. Through repeated and conscious acknowledgment of it, one cultivates tremendous inner courage. Eventually, one succeeds in detaching themselves from the fear of suffering. This fear is the source of why suffering becomes intolerable for many. We are programmed by our culture to respond to a natural and essential cycle with dread. Released of such fear, we allow ourselves to live more fully in the moment. As we become more present with suffering, we are better able to embrace the joyous moments as they come. Of course, this truth was long ago noted by the Buddha and adopted as a way of life by Bodhisattvas. Despite the West's growing interest in Eastern thought, this approach is still foreign to a culture that perceives suffering and joy as dueling counterparts.

"Illusion of Separation"
To separate joy from sadness
Is like:
Removing water from life
In the end:
Body and soul both suffer
Wither away
And die.

Universal Truth Four: We are ALL ONE

Evidence of oneness abounds. It can be experienced on a walk into nature where the river, rocks, mountains, and trees coalesce to form one majestic painting. Oneness also finds expression through our hollowed guides--- the sun and moon.

Perhaps you had an experience when you felt connected. Maybe you were dreaming of a close friend, but awoke suddenly, to check the time on your phone. Surprisingly, you received a message from the person you had dreamt about. Or, possibly, you arrived at a perfect understanding with an animal during a divine moment of interaction. In these times, we acknowledge that all sentient beings vibrate as one. In fact, scientific research now lends support to what spiritual teachers have been saying for centuries.

Within the emerging field of theoretical physics, preliminary research shows that all molecular particles in the universe are linked together by tiny, microscopic strings. These strings, theorists like Michio Kaku posit, are infinitely smaller than that of atoms. The hypothesis, known as M-theory, is the latest breakthrough that attempts to reconcile Einstein's unified field theory - essentially a theory for everything in the universe. Such a finding would only confirm our natural state of oneness.

TRUTH IS SUBJECTIVE

In addition to the four universal truths, is the truth arrived through self- reflection. As eloquently captured by Plato in *The Trial and Death of Socrates*, truth is subjective. One arrives at it through their own direct experiences. For example, take a controversial issue like police brutality. Those who have been its victims are likely to arrive at this truth: police officers are cruel and oppressive people. However, those who grew up with an officer as a friend or relative, would arrive at a radically different perception: police are benevolent workers out to protect society.

Which is the truth then? Are police officers the Anti-Christ personified? Or, are they superheroes in blue? It all depends on who's doing the perceiving. As is the case with most of us, the "truth" usually lies somewhere in between. As a collective unit, the chief function of police forces are (unquestionably) to maintain social control for the benefit of the governing class. In the furtherance of these objectives, they are given the power to use violence. Does such a description fit with the police as oppressor narrative? Absolutely. It may also be the case that not all individual police officers act with cruel intent.

To claim to "know" the truth can be a very tricky and dangerous business. It has been the catalyst of both religious and political wars; and has spurred on countless genocides of our own brothers and sisters. As a rule of thumb, never trust an individual or an organized collective who say they know the truth and especially do not be fooled when that same person or group claims to be "wise" for "knowing" it. Maybe you will find these words I wrote helpful:

"When times get rough, too often we fail to consult our soul's intention. Instead, we latch on to the words of a self-described "expert or "guru." Let me help you," proclaims the expert. "Follow my path and you will achieve success," promises the guru. Why would a truly wise person claim to "know" the right path? To be sure, those who have obtained some knowledge into the mysteries of creation ask the right questions. The right questions induce the soul into a contemplation of its very own being. But there is no such thing as a right answer. Each of us has a uniquely divine path back to the same source of oneness.

Aside from asking the right questions, the wise man is also a compassionate observer of human activity. In others, he observes all that he studies within himself: their patterns of behavior, the nature of their sustained interactions, and the threads that tie people together in their worship of God. The person of wisdom does this so that they may come to a fuller understanding of both the joys and hardships of life. Only in drawing upon their own direct experiences, does the true holder of wisdom share their perspectives with humanity. Then, and only then, are they prepared to impart knowledge. Crucially, the sharing of it is always done with the intent to uplift and inspire—not to condescend down to and discourage. Nor does a wise being push their beliefs onto any other. How can they possibly know the subjectivity that is truth?

It follows, then, that a true person of wisdom does not judge the opinions of any other. Nor does he/she condemn one's uniquely held perspectives. For they, too, were arrived at through the same avenue of direct experience. Finally, the seeker of truth silently imparts this knowledge to all who are blessed to cross their path:

Trust in the inner words of your own knowing. They will never lead you astray. The God from within knows nothing of the game that Charlatans play. Deep in the foundation of IT's purity, lies a humbleness that transcends the ways of deception. The God from within only speaks the language of honesty and love."

The values of cooperation, faith, unity, and truth, will pave the way for the spiritual revolution that is just now underway. In so doing, we will emancipate ourselves from the yoke that ego brings: enslavement and oppression, alienation and sadness, anger and violence. We will finally evolve into the loving and compassionate family that we were always meant to be. Yet, one substantial question still remains - how will we get "there?" For some, having faith renders this question meaningless. If it is our destiny to evolve spiritually, then it will inevitably happen when it is time.

There are others, however, who would like to help move this process along. These "earth activists" cite some of the urgent environmental problems we now face such as: the deterioration of our global water supply, deforestation, climate change, and the impact of massive environmental catastrophes on our ecosystems. They argue that if we don't purge humanity of its egoistic ways now, we may wind up destroying our only home. Fortunately, there is much we can do to expedite our own evolution. Our actions must be guided by spirit.

Part III. A Road Map for the Spiritual Revolution

There are three phases of the spiritual revolution that are already happening simultaneously. The first phase may be the most challenging as it relates to the liberation of one's soul from social conditioning. I say, the "most challenging," because one has to come to this on their own. As the great spiritual teacher, Ram Dass, noted, "one cannot set out to heal the suffering of others, if they have not yet freed themselves from their own worlds of self-delusion." This explains why so many protest movements in the past became muddled in the abyss of self-righteous reaction. The activists tried to change the world without first turning their lens inwards. The consequence? Many such movements became further expressions of ego. For a historical case in point, refer to the early (and tense) exchanges between hippies and returning soldiers from Vietnam.

Establishing revolutionary mediums is the second phase of the spiritual revolution. I am concerned here with the sharing of one's unique insights with others. Every effort should be made to spread these values to anyone whose heart is open to the message of peace, unity, and love. At our core, we are all spiritual beings. Due to the soul crushing nature of society, many of us have just forgotten who we really are. It is all our jobs to help remind each other.

Finally, in phase three, we will begin to establish the external features of the new society. I use the term "external features" to refer to the diversity of living models that we will adopt collectively. Examples include: the return back to small economies of scale, the rapid re-emergence of intentional communities, and the introduction of direct democracy. Below, are detailed accounts of each of these three evolutionary phases.

Part III Section 1: The Liberation of the Soul

If our species is to find relief from suffering, we must heal ourselves first. After all, it is people themselves who staff and serve the structures that perpetuate human misery. Societal institutions are reflections of our individual states of consciousness. Healing as a species requires that we turn inwards. This is not so easy to accomplish. Particularly, when we are talking over 7 billion people globally! Thankfully, our species has been blessed through the ages by the teachings of holy sages. They include figures like: Buddha, Jesus Christ, Krishna, and Mohammad. They also extend to the saintly wisdom of Earth's true guardians: The Indigenous peoples of the world. To this grouping, we might also add the great spiritual teachers of modern times who have offered their own insights into ending human suffering.

Here are brief descriptions of some of these inner pathways. To this list, I have also added my own suggestions from personal practice. They should be taken with a grain of salt. What has worked for me, may not wind up working for you.

RIGHT MIND/ATTITUDE

One must first make the conscious choice to turn inwards. Countless circumstances may arise that alter one's state of being. For some people, self-exploration begins with a persistent feeling that life is empty, hollow, or devoid of meaning. In other instances, one is forced to look inwards following a difficult set of circumstances. Examples include: the death of a loved one, divorce, or personal illness. Still, for others, a mystical experience may encourage introspection. Whatever the catalyst may be, it is inevitable that the unconscious soul will awake from its slumber.

Time Spent in Nature

"How important is a constant intercourse with nature
and the contemplation of natural phenomena to the
preservation of moral and intellectual health."

-HENRY DAVID THOREAU-

One finds peace in the majesty of nature. It is difficult not to feel part of something greater when roaming the woods or swimming in the ocean. It is remarkable how all of the natural world exists in total and complete harmony. Mankind can learn much about peace from the Earth. One also becomes more still through time spent in the natural world. In silence, we are gently guided inwards to our true essence of soul.

<u>Suggested practice:</u> Try going out on nature walks 3-4 days a week. Take at least half of your hikes solo. The solitude will help you become more silent. You will be surprised at how much time you spend reflecting. On these walks, place all your regrets about the past and concerns over the future to rest. Focus all your energies on the beauty that surrounds you. Feel the vibrations of the rocks and trees. Marvel at the sacred water in the creek. Fall to your knees in homage to the ground below you.

You may substitute activities like swimming, biking, or rock climbing for hiking, if that is what you prefer. Time spent in nature can take many forms. Finally, make it a habit to carry a journal or notepad with you into the woods. You may find it useful for recording your thoughts and revelations.

MEDITATION/PRAYER

One's natural tendency for compassion is activated through meditation and prayer. Through the practice, one also becomes more adept at being in the present moment. Meditation/prayer also fosters an intimate connection to God. It helps affirm the oneness of our existence. *Suggested practice:* three days a week, for periods of 15-20 minutes, try siting in a posture that is comfortable for you (Indian style pose or sitting in chair). Close your eyes and begin the meditation by focusing on your breath. Breathing is the phenomenon that links each of the three aspects of your being: mind, body, and soul.

One breathing exercise you could try is to imagine your "happy place". If you can't think of one, envision a calm ocean wave gliding gently into shore on the inhale breath and going back out on the exhale breath. You may also enjoy a love and kindness meditation. In this technique, one harnesses their energy with the intent of sending good will to another being(s). The aim is to relieve suffering and promote healing. In a love and kindness meditation, picture pink light from the Universe filling your heart with love on the inhale breath. Then on the out breath, imagine that light seeping out of your heart in a series of waves to the intended being(s) of your affection. Your body will feel light and charged during this meditation. No energy is stronger than love.

CREATIVE EXPRESSION

Creative expression is another practice that heals one's soul. In the act of creating, one channels the divine energies of Oneness. Creative expression may take several forms including (but not limited to): music, writing, drawing/painting, graphic design, photography, or dancing. Whatever outlet you choose, be sure that your soul derives great satisfaction from it. _Suggested practice:_ Those who act upon their creativity (it is innate in all of us) feel inspired. Inspiration is the great catalyst of creative expression. The question then becomes how does one find inspiration?

Some of the following practices can help one become inspired: daily walks in nature (see above), meditation/prayer (see also above), and the smoking of ganja when sitting down to create. Each guides us inwards. The special importance attached to the natural world and meditation have already been mentioned. Something, then, must be said for the link between marijuana and creativity. Recent studies have established direct ties between cannabis and creative expression. This means, that the scientific community is just now uncovering what artists, musicians, and writers have long known.

So before sitting down to create, try smoking a little bit of ganja out of a bowl, pipe, joint, or whatever mode you feel most comfortable. As a rule of thumb, try not to over indulge. Translation: do not take copious bong hits and then expect to go create! This will not help your cause! Instead, try smoking just enough (maybe a couple hits in all) until you start feeling creative. But not so much that your mind feels hazy. Combining walks in nature with meditation and ganja (you can try all three together!) should activate some of that bottled-up inspiration that Dominant Culture works so hard to keep dormant.

Ganja/Psychedelics

Back in the 1960's, the hippies had a love affair with both ganja and psychedelics. Turns out, those of today do too! If used with purpose, both can be quite useful in liberating one's self from cultural conditioning. Under their "influence" we become aware of our thoughts, intentions, and actions. This is the crucial point that separates both from substances like alcohol, cocaine, and the various prescription pills on the market. Whereas the latter provide exterior distractions from one's inner state of being, the former provide gateways into it. To group "drugs" like ganja with substances like alcohol is absurd. For the one has very real and mystical uses spiritually, while the other is rancorous to the human spirit.

Suggested practices: try smoking small amounts of ganja during a hike, before a meditation, or while creating. The idea is to make the association in your mind between ganja and spirituality. You may find yourself smoking every day or even many times throughout. The same should not be said for psychedelics. They are NOT to be used every day. Psychedelics should be used sparingly. When one makes the choice to trip, they should take great care in selecting a calm environment for the event. Tripping with a small group of trusted companions (1 or 2) is also advised. For more detail about the psychedelic experience, and on what to expect, refer back to the essay "Psychedelic Encounters with Spirit".

Connecting with Community

The importance in finding what Buddhists call a "Sangha", or a community of fellow seekers, cannot be overstated. The community does not have to be large. It can be comprised of as few as three to four people. The idea is to surround yourself with kind and humble people who are at similar junctures as you on their journey. Grow and learn from one another. That is how we evolve.

Suggestions:

Do not search for a spiritual community. Let it blossom naturally. Nothing, however, should stop you from sending out this intent to the Universe. In due time, you will notice how the right people just seem to drift into your life at the perfect moment. At first, you may regard their appearances as coincidental. Overtime, you will come to see them as divinely placed.

Finding Time in Solitude

"Life is an island in an ocean of solitude and seclusion".

-KAHIL GIBRAN-

Humans were not meant to be alone. Nor were we intended to spend the good part of our time in the company of others. Providing ample opportunity for solitude is as crucial to one's inner journey as that of building community. We have our best moments of reflection when we are in seclusion. Everyone has experienced periods of deep contemplation while riding solo on a long car trip, or while showering. Perhaps you have pondered the meaning of life while on a walk through the woods. Personal reflection is the life force behind one's spiritual journey.

Suggestions: Put aside one hour per day just for you. I personally like mornings. For others, it may be evenings or afternoons. Spend that hour in solitude and focus all your energy on being with yourself. Detach from life's distractions and shut off your television, cell phone, and computer. Sit down on your couch and journal for a little while. Go on a solo hike in the woods. Maybe you could pick up your guitar or bongos and play. If you are a sculptor get to work molding that clay! You could also spend an hour in meditation/prayer. The idea is to make your time as soulfully enriching as possible. Over time, you will find great fulfillment in just being alone.

Spending Time with Animals

As my own path continues to unfold, I have gained an appreciation for the role that my dog (Abbie) has played. The way that I see her is just as an old friend described her own relationship with her dog: "I sincerely believe that my dog is a mirror onto myself." If we want to learn about the state of our soul, one thing we can all do is to observe our close animal friends. The bonds between human and animal are powerful and enduring and gives both the ability to take on each other's energy. This is particularly true for dogs and cats, but also applies to other animals like cows and horses. If one's pet is happy and content, that usually means that you are happy and content. Both of your souls are strong. If your animal is a bit anxious or on edge, then the first question you should ask yourself is: "Am I anxious and on edge"?

Aside from providing "mirrors onto the self," the vast intuitive powers of animals alone provide daily instructions in awareness. For a case in point: observe a dog or cat in the moments before a storm. Watch as the animal grows nervous well before their human tunes in to the shifting weather. Most scientists attribute the intuitive abilities of animals to mere "instinct". To a certain degree that may be true. Something deeper is also at play. Animals seem to be much more attuned to the vibrations of the earth than are most humans. One could say that animals are endowed with great spiritual powers. What they may lack in what we humans call "reason", they more than make up for in spirit power. They are our sacred messengers.

Suggestions: If your thoughts are ever heavy or you are enduring a period of suffering, go sit with your pet and give him/her a hug. Sit with them in silence for 10-15 minutes. You may be surprised at how calm this interaction makes you feel. This will allow you to quiet your mind and turn inwards. If you do not own a pet (or even if you do) try going for a walk in the woods. Walk silently and just observe the wild life. I firmly believe that the Native Americans are correct when they say that animals deliver existential messages. So, if on that walk, you encounter a deer who bows its head to you (numerous times), listen closely. Its message will surely resonate with your soul!

READING

Reading for the sake of reading is never a bad thing. From this activity alone, we derive knowledge about the world and other cultures, engender new neurons in our brains, and ward off grave ailments like Alzheimer's disease. Reading can also be of use to us spiritually. Over the past couple of years, each new book that has found me has been of immense value to my journey. The messages derived seem to mirror the juncture of the path that I am on. In the context of one's own search, spiritual writing should always serve two intertwined functions: to give expression to that which our soul intuitively knows, and to share insights that may help another along his/her path. In the end, all spiritual books should convey the message of universal love.

Suggestions: When the mood strikes.... take the time to read any book that speaks to your soul. Try to read in a quiet place and without distractions.

PART III: SECTION 2: MEDIUMS OF THE REVOLUTIONARY MESSAGE

The dissemination of the revolutionary message is the second phase of the spiritual revolution. As of yet, we have not reached anywhere close to a critical mass of awakening souls. Keep the faith. It will inevitably happen. In the meantime, we have the power to shape how quickly (or slowly) we move along in this evolutionary process. The airing of the message begins with each individual's day to day actions. There is much we can all do to spread peace and love to others. We must remember that the collective consciousness of mankind is comprised from each and every person's present state of awareness. In other words, we all leave an imprint with our thoughts, intentions, and actions. It follows, that we can all be messengers in this most inspiring of journeys.

The Medium of Kindness

In your daily interactions, try holding the door open for another. This is a simple but common practice in places like the Southern United States, where door holding is seen as a friendly gesture of respect and acknowledgment. In that region, people hold doors in workplaces, at restaurants, and even at bars. It is also an action that conveys cooperation, as both the door holder and the benefactor swap roles when walking through the next door together.

Another subtle but profound act of kindness is embedded in an anecdotal story. As recounted in "The Mystical Experience of Love", I had the opportunity to befriend an Anthropology professor named Jethro. I have many fond memories of him, but one in particular stands out. Jethro used to discuss the daily act that he derived most meaning from. Each day, he made it a point to acknowledge passing strangers and acquaintances with eye contact, a friendly smile, and a warm hello. He would practice this art in the hallways and cafeteria of the college, and on the way to and from his car. Curious, I would always ask him how many people responded, and in what fashion. On the best of days, he would recall, maybe 4 out of 10 people would greet him back with a brief hello. Two people would return his hello with a smile. Tellingly, only one person would establish eye contract with him, smile, and say hello!

Remarkably though, Jethro was not discouraged by the seeming lack of reciprocity. To him, one sincere acknowledgment was enough to inspire (in his own words) "faith in the human race for one hundred years." Eye contact was not only a sign of acknowledgment for Jethro, but a glimpse into their very being. He had a fondness of saying, "the eyes can't hide what is deep inside one's soul." Making eye contact when acknowledging a stranger is among the kindest acts one can bestow upon another. There are countless other ways we can be kind in our daily interactions. Here are three more:

- Providing change or foodstuffs to a homeless person. Not out of pity, but because our soul knows that it is the right thing to do
- Helping a stranded motorist on the side of the road. You help that person jumpstart their car because you empathize with them
- Participating in a neighborhood-wide search for a missing pet. You sympathize with both the owner and the missing animal and you do whatever is possible to help

In each of these common scenarios, the revolutionary values of cooperation, faith, unity, and truth are present.

The Medium of Reverence for the Natural World

We can also convey new societal values through showing reverence for the natural world. For Gary Zukav, author of the book <u>Seat of the Soul,</u> reverence is an attitude of honoring life. It is engaging in a depth of contact with existing that is beyond our attachments to the physical world. To practice reverence is to acknowledge the spirit that lies in each and every being. How do we cultivate this respect for nature in our day to day lives? We begin by paying careful attention to our lifestyle choices and habits. One does not have to live in the mountains or work on a farm to learn how to respect the Earth. Toward these ends, try introducing some of the following practices into your day to day life:

- When you go to the grocery store, try using reusable instead of plastic bags.
- For all the cell phone users (my self-included) try to resist the "upgrade" mania that prompts users to discard perfectly functioning

devices for flashier gadgets. Keep in mind that abandoned cell phones wind up polluting the earth with its harmful toxins. In the grand scheme of things, there really is no difference between the "old school" flip phone and the ever popular iPhone. Both put one in contact.

* Consider cutting your showers in half. Instead of a 20-30-minute wash try reducing it to no more than 10 minutes. (something I very badly struggle with).
* If you are unwinding on a boat, try bringingThe beer cans (instead of glass) and leave no trace. Glass bottles commonly wind up broken and present a potential harm to wildlife and even household pets!

These are just a few ways that people can show reverence for the natural world. Through cultivating a deep reverence for nature, one is also acknowledging a universal truth: all living beings are one.

The Medium of Creative Expression

A painting caught my eye one day as I roamed through an art museum in Nashville, Tennessee. The artwork was a depiction of the internal human body. Rather than portray its skeletal features, the artist conveyed the energy or chakra points of the being. The body was painted the colors of the primary seven access points, and depicted waves of energy (of the same colors) flowing into and out from the body. The message of the painting was clear: our true essence is found in the higher spiritual realms.

If one painting has the ability to deliver truth, then so does one song, photo, or poem. As more of us continue to awaken, we will feel an insatiable desire to share our insights with others. The soul's vehicle of communication becomes creative expression. It can take many forms. Painting, drawing, sculpting, music, and writing are among the most popular modes, but by no means the only ones.

Music is a key outlet of spiritual expression. As discussed in the "Hippie Revival", entire genres of music such as reggae, folk, blue grass, and Indigenous music serve as powerful mediums for the soul. For example, my good friends from the Nashville based reggae band, Roots of a Rebellion, emphasize the themes of cooperation, faith, unity, and the attainment of truth in their songs. In so doing, they serve as conduits of an eternal message. Remarkably, there are even musicians who convey this same love without the need for words. The ambient composer, Karunesh, is one such example. As is the Native American composer, R. Carlos Nakai. With album titles (between them) like, "Call of the Mystic," "Global village", "Earth Spirit", and "Sanctuary", one can feel their spiritual odysseys through music.

The written word, too, is an effective channel for the spiritual revolution. After all, some of the most inspiring books in history have been works about awakening. The <u>Bhagavad Gita</u>, The <u>Upanishads</u>, The <u>Bible</u>, and The <u>Koran</u> are all examples. As are more modern works of writing, such as Kahlil Gibran's <u>The Prophet</u>, Herman Hesse's <u>Siddhartha</u>, Henry David Thoreau's <u>Walden</u>, Walt Whitman's *Leaves of Grass*, and Ram Dass's <u>Be Here Now</u>. The spirit behind each of these works are eternal.

Poetry, too, is a unique and inspired form of written expression. For it provides a direct pathway into one's experience of reality. Poetry also conveys in a few short lines what it takes entire books to write. Its brevity is a reflection of its heartfelt sincerity. As a pure expression of soul, one can express deeply felt truths through this medium. It is intimately personal, but also speaks to all journeys upon the path. As an example, consider how clearly the cosmic theme of oneness shines through in each of the personal narratives down below. The poems, by Nancy Wood, were written in the spirit of the Pueblo Indians of North America:

Untitled One
My help is in the mountain
Where I take myself to heal
The earthly wounds

That people give to me
I find a rock with sun on it
And a stream where the water runs gentle
And the trees which one by one give me company.
So I must stay for a long time
Until I have grown from the rock
And the stream is running through me
And I cannot tell myself from one tall tree.
Then I know that nothing touches me
Nor makes me run away,
My help is in the mountain
That I take away with me.

Untitled Two

I have killed the deer.
I have crushed the grasshopper
And the plants he feeds upon.
I have cut through the heart
Of trees growing old and straight.
I have taken fish from water
And birds from the sky.
In my life I have needed death
So that my life can be.
When I die I must give life.
To what has nourished me.
The earth receives my body
And gives it to the plants
And to the caterpillars
To the birds
And to the coyotes
Each in its own turn so that
The circle of life is never broken.

The Medium of Teaching: Old Forms and New

Teaching is the art of sharing one's knowledge with another. It finds its form in what we call "insights" and reflects perspectives gleaned from one's own direct experience. To be a teacher does not imply that one is necessarily teaching "truth". For that which is being shared, only represents one's conception of reality. This is why the best teachers---that is, the most humble--- stray away from providing answers, opting instead to ask questions.

The desire to teach springs from the soul's yearning to connect with fellow beings. As it is birthed from such a passion, teaching is an act of compassion. If our essence is love, and reverence for both self and others is its expression, then we all have the ability to be teachers. This ancient art flows from one's soul. To access the teacher from within is to acknowledge one's divine self. It must also be said that the act of teaching transcends both constraints of time and space. It does not require a set period or designated place to meet in order to transmute knowledge. Teaching, then, cannot be confined to the formal channels of-institutionalized "learning" that society reveres. Nor, can its soulful expression be converted into an occupation that is com modified and packaged as "education". Teaching is a noble craft spun of the finest wools.

At the present time, humanity is entering upon a new period of knowledge sharing. An age that reflects the twin flames of the soul: love and faith. Many among us are already combining the traditional models of teaching with its fresh and dynamic forms. The result? The revolutionary message is reaching a growing population in unconventional and inspiring ways.

Today, there are multiple platforms for the modern teacher. The more traditional pathways of formal-occupational teaching do still exist as effective mediums. It is true, that the modern education system (from Kindergarten-higher education) has become little more than an indoctrination machine. There are still, however, plenty of teachers who share a genuine interest in the cultivation of spirit. This kind of teacher finds a way to facilitate inner exploration in their classroom. They do so without regard for the subject they teach, or for whom they are teaching. The in-spired literature teacher facilitates discussion on themes like cooperation and faith through books, just as the Geology professor encourages one's reverence for the natural world through his/her lectures about stones.

The renewed interest (in the west) in meditation has also given birth to a new breed of spiritual teachers. Many of whom hail from the vari-ous schools of Buddhism (such as Zen or Theravada). Others emphasize nature in their teachings. Some teachers even ground their meditation classes in multiple philosophical frameworks. People are searching for a new message. One that matches the openness and sincerity of their own soul. The growing interest in meditation is a very positive phenomenon and effective medium for silently communicating the revolutionary mes-sage of awakening.

Like the 1960's-70's, informal gatherings of people are also springing up from the grassroots to spread the seeds of peace, unity, and love. In these groups, there is no leader or figure whom the meeting or event is centered around. These small, but intimate spaces emerge spontaneously and often within the structures of the formal conditioning outlets them-selves. They extend meaning to the common activist phrase: "building the new society within the shell of the old."

In my second stint as a college professor, I had the grateful experience to have shared in the formation of such a space on campus. We called this twice weekly event a "peace gathering." Every week, Betty (another instructor and co-creator of the group), myself, and anywhere between 2 to 12 students, would meet in my office for an hour of silence. Each peace gathering began with brief introductions. Eventually, we progressed to ask questions such as: "what is one thing you are grateful for"? After 5-10 minutes, we were all invited to share our poetry, writing, or art. This period of sharing was fascinating, because it provided insights into how others express themselves. At one such gathering, Rose even read one of her poems, which astounded. On a different day, a comic book illustrator displayed his art work for us. After people were finished sharing, Betty and I would (on separate days) facilitate a 20-35-minute guided meditation.

As the weekly gatherings grew more comfortable, the line between Betty, I, and the students grew exceedingly thin. In our peaceful hour together, it became unclear who the teachers were. Then one day it dawned on me...we were all each other's teachers! Gatherings similar to the type held at my former college are even popping up in those places more known for their strict religiosity. The growth in these types of spaces are a testament to the power of the human spirit. It also indicates the blossoming of a fresh and healthy perspective. For in our species' moment of becoming, each of us are teachers. Gone are the days of the shepherd and his sheep.

PART III SECTION 3: RIGHTEOUS REVOLUTION

At the present time, much of the human species are guided by the egoistic values of competition, fear, separation, and ignorance. In turn, each of these false senses of self are reflected by powerful (and intertwined) societal structures that form an "Unholy Alliance" of organized religion, the state, and capitalism. Collectively speaking, each are so ingrained in our lives, that they find expression in the following (and familiar) institutional forms: the church, government, and the corporation. This "Unholy Alliance," represents mankind's collective projection of ego. For the planet's well-being, it is our duty to break down these structures. The tactics we use to resist them must be peaceful. Matching violence with violence only begets more violence. For too long, our human family has been trapped in this soul crushing pattern of reaction. It has led to endless suffering and bloodshed. It has also frustrated our attempts at unity. The more we turn to violence to solve injustice, the greater the suffering we perpetuate. Look to the long-standing conflict between the State of Israel and the Palestinian People for a dramatic case in point.

Most significantly, the use of violence also violates the ultimate aspirations of all serious spiritual faiths: peace, unity, and love. Anytime one takes the life of any other (in instances of non-self-defense) they are dishonoring the gift of existing, perpetuating the myth of separation, and living in ignorance to that great universal truth that we are all one.

The spiritual revolution does not end with the peaceful dissolution of the "Unholy Alliance." The three structures must be replaced at the grass-roots by new societal features. Ones that reflect the moral values of the new society. I use the word "feature" to imply that it is not beneficial for us to build new structures in its place. The very notion of the term "structure" should lead us all to ponder the following question: has this "Unholy Alliance" progressed us spiritually? What follows below, is a meditation upon this question.

STRUCTURES OF EGO

ORGANIZED RELIGION

Organized religion is a man-made foundation built on fear and the submission of one's soul to authority. It is the misapplication of the teachings of such transcendental figures as Jesus and Mohammad for the purposes of wielding power. Organized religion presents a potential illusion for spiritual seekers. Because of this, one must not be blinded by the righteous sounding rhetoric of religious authorities.

Organized religion embodies each of the four egoistic principles. From its earliest days, the church has always regarded differing faiths (to their own) as competition. The mainstream factions of Christianity, Islam, and Judaism (and to a much lesser extent, Hinduism and Buddhism) each share in the belief that there is only one "true" pathway to God. It follows that all alternative paths are dismissed as blasphemous. This outlook is dangerous as it envisions a world of "us" and "them," "saved" and "unsaved;" "infidel" vs "believer". This injection of competition into mankind's search for God has been historically used to justify barbaric acts against our brothers and sisters. A small sampling includes: the Crusades, the genocide of indigenous peoples in both North and South America, and the African slave trade. Competition also breeds separation. Currently, the major organized religions of the world are arrayed against one another. In reality, all should be joining together in what they have in common: a belief in a higher set of moral principles.

Sadly, this separation between faiths has only produced mass intolerance. As modern day examples, look no further than Christian fundamentalists' hostile attitudes toward Muslims, or of the Islamic fundamentalists' (equally) aggressive tones toward Christians. In citing these examples, it is important to note that the mystical wings of both Christianity (Christian Mysticism) and Islam (Sufism) have long condemned separation as a construct of ego. Instead, Christian and Sufi mystics have long called for interfaith dialogue and unity.

Organized religion also cultivates an element of fear within its consortium of priests, rabbis, and clerics. In turn, religious authorities pass on these teachings to their attendees, flock, and the like. The way that fear is packaged to its followers will deviate from church to church and from denomination to denomination. The general message, however, is always the same: the priest, the rabbi, the cleric, etc., stands as the intermediary between God and the people. By adhering to the priest's (rabbi, cleric, etc.) prescribed for teachings, one might escape God's wrath and secure a seat in heaven.

Aside from being informed of their "sinful" nature, worshipers also are taught that God is a vengeful being who can only be appeased through a series of detached and archaic rituals. It is easy to see how such a belief system might make for a frightened and paranoid people. Many followers of organized religion come to view the world as an "evil" place. Of course, this "evil" must be cleansed by the self-righteous gracing of their own faith. Born of such fear, the major organized religions of the world perpetuate an ignorance into the true state of our being. Absent from their narratives, are descriptions of the divine miracle of life, of which humans are just a very miniscule part.

THE STATE

The state is a systematic organization of violence that protects the rich and powerful from the poor and downtrodden. It acquires its power through assuming a monopoly over the legitimate use of violence. This means that the state claims the right to use force (for example, imprisonment, seizure of property, the death penalty) while prohibiting the people from doing so. Unlike the rest of us, the state does not have to toil for its sustenance. It secures its wealth through the labor it extracts (see steals) from others via taxes.

In order to secure its grip on power, the state employs an enormous fleet of enforcers, aimed at quashing any resistance from the public, should it arise. The state's hired "guns" serve various functions toward this end, and include: armed officials (for example the police and national security forces like the FBI and Homeland security), politicians (the law making apparatus for the state), bureaucrats (those who staff its many bureaus and agencies), and elite academics (a tiny but ambitious group of elite intellectuals who lend their brains with the hopes of acquiring prestige). The state goes to great lengths to maintain the steady flow of unearned wealth into their coffers. These "efforts" often take the form of unspeakable acts of cruelty against humanity and nature.

Like organized religion, the state too, adheres to an egoistic framework. It regards the power of its own citizenry and rival states as competition to its hold on power. Because it relates to other governments and people this way, it rules from a position of fear. The state's paranoia is reflected in its constant resort to violence when it is in dispute with another "rival." The state's propensity for conflict results in either war overseas or tyrannical rule at home. The state lives in such fear of a domestic revolt that it conjures up "enemies" so as to keep its citizenry in a constant state of paranoia. In so doing, the state unifies the people around its illusionary role as their great "protector." The United States Government's post 9/11 campaign of fear is an example of such propaganda in action.

Through its invention of "enemies" overseas, the state also exasperates global disunity among all the Earth's children. However, its promotion of separation does not end here. Because it fears its own populace, it plays on artificial divisions between the people. The state bestows special privileges among some portions of the population while withholding them from others. The state also deliberately stokes conflict between race, gender, and socioeconomic groups. They do so in order to divert attention from the very real problems that flow from the exercise of state power. The reality, of course, is that there are no divisions between humans. They are mere constructs of the ego.

The state may also be said to perpetuate ignorance. As most education and media outlets are under the control (directly or indirectly) of the state, people are kept in the dark about the true nature of their governments. Sadly, many are shocked when they later discover their long list of crimes against humanity. Until we peacefully dismantle the crime syndicate known as the State, we will see more of the same at the collective level: great suffering among all God's people.

CAPITALISM

Capitalism is an economic system predicated on the mass consumption of natural resources like water, trees, and rubber. It could be described as a sophisticated model of collective exploitation, whereby a small minority of people profit off the treasures of the natural world and from each other. This mentality of exploitation is seen in each of the key phases of capitalist "enterprise". The process begins with the extraction of resources from nature. It then progresses to the production stage. At this phase, the business owner(s) hire workers to build or create their products. However, there is a catch. The workers are paid much less than their real labor value. This is done to generate profit for the capitalist owner(s). After the product is assembled and packaged, it is then brought to market by a second group of workers called distributors. They, too, are paid far below the real cost of their labor value. Finally, the product reaches you the consumer!

Capitalism shares a crucial and foundational piece with the first two structures of the "Unholy Alliance," which is guided by egoistic values. Through the system of capitalism, the chief officers of a Fortunate 500 corporation (today's dominant capitalist entity) are conditioned to regard all other companies in their sphere of the "market" as "rivals," and all "rival" companies present a threat to one's own profit margins. The successful corporation is thus ruthless in how it addresses its competition. The bigger a capitalist enterprise grows; the better adept it becomes at controlling it. A whole range of options exist to control competitors: push them out of business by undercutting prices, buy out the competition through mergers and acquisitions, and enlist the help of the state to rig the markets for them through an assortment of laws and regulations.

Competition is also present within the walls of the capitalist companies themselves. Employees are regularly pitted against one another for raises, promotions, and increased authority. This competition geared environment engenders great fear in the workers. When the times call for it, capitalist "enterprisers" do not hesitate to make the "tough choices." The workers' fear of being laid off serves the capitalist well. With the threat of termination, the worker is more willing to toil longer hours for lesser wages.

Through the deep inequality it creates between the rich and poor, capitalism also breeds separation. Due to its pervasive influence, we now commonly reference one another by the positions we occupy in the capitalist pecking order. For example, many of us have heard the following insinuations: "Suzy is middle class, and married up to Ben who is in the upper class." Or, "Greg is quite well to do. He is an engineer." The truth is that we are not separated by such superficial distinctions. We are all seeds born of the same and humble Creator.

Aside from dividing us from one another, capitalism also creates a false line of demarcation between mankind and nature. By not honoring the wonder that is the natural world, we advance the fantasy that humans stand front and center of creation. As long as we adopt a system that thrives off unchecked resource extraction and consumption, we will continue to lurk in the dark shadow of ignorance. How is it possible to separate oneself from that which sustains you? Our "captains of industry," "statesmen," and "religious authorities" will no doubt make a competing claim: that the natural world was intended for us to do with as we please. The human spirit knows better. Deep down, it acknowledges that nature and man are one.

Resisting the *"Unholy Alliance"*

"Like every great religion of the past we seek to find the divinity within and to express this revelation in a life of glorification and the worship of God. These ancient goals we define in the metaphor of the present—turn on, tune in, drop out".

-TIMOTHY LEARY-

Back in 1967, Leary delivered these inspiring words to over 30,000 hippies at Golden Gate Park in San Francisco, California. Packed in his now iconic phrase, "Turn on, tune in, drop out," is a profound message about the coming of awareness and how one should interact with the madness of the outside world. Leary's suggestion to the hippie youth: find an inner refuge in God (for him, through psychedelics) and divorce oneself from attachments to mainstream culture.

Though spoken nearly 50 years ago, Leary's message provides a road map for dismantling the "Unholy Alliance "of today. First, we need to "turn on." That is, we need to become aware of the mass suffering that our culture produces. Then, we must "tune in," to our intuitive voices and ask ourselves this question: are societal structures aligned with basic spiritual principles? If the answer is no, then it is our obligation to dissolve them. Leary is clear that this should be done peacefully. A question immediately arises: how do we confront powerful institutions (in particular the state) that only react with violence? Don't engage them at all. "Drop out" from the conflict. The same way one disengages from an angry individual is also how we address organized religion, the state, and capitalism. How do we begin to "drop out" from Dominant Society? By the withholding of our support.

Through the withholding of our money, the "Unholy Alliance" could not remain in existence. Churches receive much of their income from devotees through tithing. Governments are dependent on individual tax payers for up to 60 % or more of their funding. The power of multinational corporations is tied to the consumption patterns of the people. In other words, we have the power. Through our willingness to pay, we confer legitimacy upon them.

As a growing mass of souls begin to awaken, it will become impossible to turn a blind eye to the inconsistencies between our internal and external realities. Many will feel compelled to do something to alleviate our collective suffering. Naturally, we will shift our attention to the institutional purveyors of injustice. Dissolving the "Unholy Alliance" will not put an end to all suffering. We need to build a new framework that reflects the noble aims of spirit. If we fail to replace the egoistic foundations with spiritual ones, we will just wind up with them again. Lending meaning to the popular phrase: "the more things change, the more they stay the same." A true revolution is marked by the uprooting of egoistic foundations and the planting of new peaceful ones.

An example of a true revolution is the kind that happened in Tibet between the years of 1912-1951. During this period of independence, the Tibetan people radically re-oriented their society in accord with spiritual principles. The chief aim of the society became the purification of one's soul. The Tibetans lived in this fashion up until the devastating invasion by Generally Mao's forces, cynically referred to as a "liberation". What the Tibetans started is just now beginning to go global. This development begs the question: after the dust settles, what will the features of this new society look like? Or, put in other words, how will we come to practice religion, politics, and economics?

The New Religion

The "new religion" will come to reflect the spiritual values of cooperation, faith, unity, and truth. World peace may be finally achievable. The full exploration of the human soul will become our primary purpose and occupation. The same level of attention that we currently devote to the study and mastery of the physical world will be applied to that of the spiritual one. Identification with one's own soul will take priority over that of our ego self.

As the shape of the post-revolutionary world unfolds, openness and tolerance (the building blocks of truth and unity) will come to pervade the new religion. There will be a great willingness among all to discuss and share one's insights with others. The statement that one "should never speak about religion in public" will be seen as archaic. As spiritual growth supplants consumerism as the central focus of human activity, we will find conversation on such matters difficult to avoid. When people become more comfortable discussing and sharing their faith with others, the traditional places we worship will also shift as well. A greater emphasis will be placed on the sacredness of the natural world.

Tolerance will also become a hallmark of the "new religion." As spiritual seekers from all walks of life continue to mingle, our acceptance of different faiths will continue to grow. Gone will be the days of religious wars and persecutions. People will come to regard divergent forms of worship as simply alternative pathways to God. Our outlook, then, will shift in attention from the superficial differences that separate the religions, to an emphasis on the core beliefs common to all. Global projects to unite all faiths, like the now global Interfaith conferences, will become the norm. Only then will the word "diversity" be spoken of genuinely.

Finally, the "new religion" will see the massive reduction of power for religious authorities. Priests, clergymen, pastors, clerics, and gurus of all stripes, will come to wield less influence over us. As our conception of the Divine moves beyond the doctrinaire portraits of IT, we will see that God is also subjective. How we come to derive meaning, depends on our own uniquely held set of beliefs, arrived at through direct experience.

THE NEW POLITICS

As the power of the state withers away under the weight of its own immorality, the many hypocrisies of its foundation will be deciphered and studied. Among the conclusions we will reach are: 1) power corrupts; 2) absolute power in the hands of one or a few individuals result(s) in barbaric acts against humanity and nature; 3) the pursuit of external power reflects the framework of ego.

Currently, politics can be thought of as an illusion. It is a game of deception that servants of the state play with the people. In a cynical ploy of our faith, the politicians set out to convince others that the interests of the state are in line with basic humanitarian values like freedom and equality. Through fancy slogans and buzzwords, appeals to jingoistic phrases and themes, and by stoking fear, they cultivate division and submission among the people. These days are soon to be over, for the spiritual revolution will usher in a "new politics."

This "new politics" will emphasize true equality and freedom of expression above all else. It will work to maintain peace and set out to resolve all conflicts nonviolently. The accumulation of external power that was the hallmark of the politics of old will no longer predominate. It will be regarded as an unfortunate relic from the past. All day to day activity of the "new politics" will take place within the sphere of one's own community and will expand no further. Politics as we know it will be recast from a framework of illusion to one that empowers.

Toward these ends, all decisions pertaining to the well-being of each community will be made by the people themselves. This model, taken from the ancient Greeks and called direct democracy, will replace the authoritarian structure of the state. Those tasked with implementing the decisions of their communities will only assume their positions for a brief tenure, as all "offices" will be rotating. Should the need arise to send representatives from one's own community to another to establish lines of trade, or to address any conflict pursuant to both parties, it is likely that those esteemed for their wisdom and humility will be selected. Further, it may come to pass, that these same representatives will also be expected to take vows of poverty and make themselves subject to a recall by the community at large. This model is predicated on the Iroquois Confederation, the 18th century agreement devised by the five (and later six) North American tribes in the Northeastern United States. In the age of "the "new politics", compassion and cooperation will come to gradually replace the state and its appendage of corrupt politicians.

The New Economics

After the spiritual revolution, a "new economics" will come to replace the exploitive capitalist system. In this new era, people will produce and trade goods of value within and outside their communities for survival, not to engage in conspicuous consumption. For the consumer based economy (that we know of) will dissolve. The philosophy of the "new economics" will display a deep reverence for nature. Great care will be taken not to disturb her natural rhythms. Should acts such as cutting down a tree for shelter or firewood be deemed necessary, that person(s) will be expected to practice the principle of ecological sustainability. That is, one does not take more from the natural world than one absolutely **needs**.

The new economy will also function at a more appropriate human scale. In other words, today's global network of corporate tyrannies will give way to drastically reduced economic units that function within communities. These units will feature small, worker managed companies called cooperatives. We might envision, then, that an alternative network of cooperatives will emerge. They will be akin to those now found in post (2003) depression Argentina.

After the spiritual revolution, we may even see the abolishment of money in many parts of the world. It is likely that the barter system (still practiced by many indigenous cultures) will be revived. The future prototype of this model may be the type found in the hippie bastion of Ithaca, New York. There, a small group of citizens have devised a system of barter called a "time bank". In it, people offer services like house cleaning or yard work. Depending on the difficulty and value (decided by the community members) of the task, one to two tokens are awarded for each completed hour of work. The recipient of the tokens may then transfer them in exchange for services from other members. In this system, the emphasis is on the exchange of goods and services, not on material acquisition.

The "new economics" will also be centered in local communities. Thus increasing the odds that both parties to an exchange will know one another personally. Such heightened levels of familiarity serve as natural bulwarks against exploitation. For one finds it more difficult to cheat their own friend or neighbor than they do a stranger. This sense of trust may evolve into an informal and grassroots system of credit. Where by, one extends it on faith alone. In the new era, we may even enjoy the emergence of gift economies. In this kind of economic exchange, one gives something of value without expecting anything in return. In a spiritual society, why couldn't "gifting" work? Like those of the new religion and politics, the new economics will come to reflect the essence of spirit in action.

THE 21ST CENTURY COMMUNE: MODEL FOR THE NEW SOCIETY

Intentional communities (referred to often as communes) may **possibly** emerge as the dominant form of social organization. Inspired by the model of tribal living practiced by the indigenous peoples of the world, communes encompass several features of the new religion, politics, and economics. A commune is an independent community of people who typically subsist off the land and live in harmony with nature. Most intentional communities are informed by spiritual values such as cooperation and non-violence. In its relation to the outside world, the commune exists as autonomously as possible. Many operate alternative energy outlets (like solar power) and grow their own food and establish (informal or formal) organizations of community aid. Some communes even erect their own alternative education systems. Contrary to mainstream associations between communes and cult leaders, most do not, in fact, revolve around only one person. Instead, power is **typically** distributed equally between its members. All have the same opportunity to participate in the decision making process.

Some communes, like The Farm, practice the Buddhist concept of "Right Livelihood". That means, one lives a life of service to others. This spirit of volunteerism has been translated into work on several humanitarian projects. These include: providing earth quake relief in Guatemala, initiating a private ambulance service for poor residents in the Bronx, New York, sending response teams to the victims of Hurricane Katrina, and inaugurating a program that introduces inner city children to the country side.

As the spiritual revolution unfolds, we can expect to see a reverse migration of sorts; a move in demographics from urban to rural areas. Once there, inspired people will begin building the infrastructure of the new society. Ideally, we would see such an explosion in the growth of new communes that systems of trade and barter would form among them. This model would only foster independence among the fledgling communes. It would also insulate them from the corrupting forces of money, that great and wretched symbol of mainstream culture. With the re-emergence of this form of living on a mass scale, people will re-learn how to embrace both self and others again.

THE SPIRITUAL REVOLUTION WILL NOT BE TELEVISED

It is our destiny as a species to evolve into the kind and compassionate beings that God intended for us all to be. As this spiritual awakening comes to pass, it is likely that many among us will not be informed of what is happening. Why won't it be known? Those who are in control of the flow of information are the very same people and structures who stand to lose power. **The spiritual revolution will not be televised!**

It is very crucial then, that we take advantage of the powerful outlets we do have, like the Internet. For our metamorphosis into conscious and loving beings will not be denied. By tuning inwards, we can also begin to feel just what is happening. To be sure, the powerful will cling to the old ways of ego. However, eventually, even they will come to "see the light." When they do, it is our responsibility as their brothers and sisters to welcome them over to the other side.

In these times, we will come to know that the unfolding of each of our personal awakenings are akin to a game of dominoes. The energy vibrations derived from each being's acknowledgment of its own self has potential to spark the same act of recognition in others. The process of coming to awareness is one of sharing and inspiring. Ultimately, humanity will reach a critical mass of awakening souls. Together, they will dissolve the societal habits and structures that have come to form our collective states of unconsciousness. In its wake, the post-revolutionary society will come into being.

Made in the USA
Middletown, DE
20 December 2017